SIDREA Series in Accounting and Business Administration

This is the official book series of SIDREA - the Italian Society of Accounting and Business Administration. This book series is provided with a wide Scientific Committee composed of Academics by SIDREA. It publishes contributions (monographs, edited volumes and proceedings) as a result of the double blind review process by the SIDREA's thematic research groups, operating at the national and international levels. Particularly, the series aims to disseminate specialized findings on several topics – classical and cutting-edge alike – that are currently being discussed by the accounting and business administration communities. The series authors are respected researchers and professors in the fields of business valuation; governance and internal control; financial accounting; public accounting; management control; gender; turnaround predictive models; non-financial disclosure; intellectual capital, smart technologies, and digitalization; and university governance and performance measurement.

Salvatore Principale

Fostering Sustainability in Corporate Governance

Analysis of the EU Sustainable Corporate Governance and Due Diligence Directives

Springer

Salvatore Principale
Sapienza University of Rome
Rome, Italy

ISSN 2662-9879 ISSN 2662-9887 (electronic)
SIDREA Series in Accounting and Business Administration
ISBN 978-3-031-30353-1 ISBN 978-3-031-30354-8 (eBook)
https://doi.org/10.1007/978-3-031-30354-8

This Springer imprint is published by the registered company Springer Nature Switzerland AG
The registered company address is: Gewerbestrasse 11, 6330 Cham, Switzerland

Preface

The company is an open system that interacts and establishes continuous relationships with the external environment. The growing complexity of the external environment, increasingly changing and competitive means that in order to be able to produce lasting value, the company must equip itself with a suitable structure to govern the continuous external changes. Corporate governance and strategic management have the leading role which must define and dictate the strategic lines by anticipating environmental changes. In this changing context, with the enlargement of the corporate boundaries, incorporating all those subjects with which the company relates, the concepts of sustainability and sustainable development have established themselves.

Sustainability can no longer be defined only as a theoretical concept reserved for a few academics. The actions undertaken by governments and regulators as well as the increasingly pressing attention of the various stakeholders are some of the drivers that in recent years have contributed to accelerating the process towards the development of a sustainable and low-emissions economy.

More than in other contexts, the European Union intends to favor the process towards a more sustainable economy adhering to the principles and objectives of sustainable development goals (SDGs) for which the Member States have committed themselves to achieve by 2030. In the last decade, the European Commission has introduced and programmed various regulations to direct the behavior of the actors of the economic system towards good practices of social and environmental sustainability. Many of these interventions concerned companies, considered fundamental and in charge of an important role in achieving the ambitious objectives of the 2030 Agenda.

In this scenario, European companies are undergoing these changes and need to govern them. Above all, companies that in the years before European policies had not been voluntarily inclined to include the values of sustainability in their strategies and policies are required to make important organizational and process changes. For example, Directive 95/2014/EU (which required the publication of a non-financial statement) has had an impact on the corporate system of all those companies that were not used to managing this information.

International organizations and scholars agree that to manage these changes well, the leadership of the company must govern these changes. Corporate governance and strategic management are considered an essential elements for integrating sustainability within the corporate system at all levels.

This book aims to analyze the relationship between governance and sustainability in light of the regulatory interventions on Sustainable Corporate Governance. The objective is to identify the challenges posed by sustainability and to evaluate through initial empirical research the state of the art of companies in the field of human rights due diligence and the governance determinants that have influenced good practices.

Starting from an analysis of the literature in order to highlight the latest evolutionary trends on the subject, this book aims to investigate the changes in governance models of companies that legislation and sustainability are imposing. Using mixed, quantitative, and qualitative methodologies, it is proposed to investigate the state of the art of European companies regarding the implementation of due diligence systems and evaluate the critical governance mechanisms to encourage the adoption of good practices to identify and prevent harmful phenomena in human rights.

The book consists of four chapters. The first chapter defines corporate governance and retraces the main theoretical frameworks underlying the conceptualization of corporate governance. Subsequently, some governance models widespread in the main European countries are proposed with a final focus on risk control and management systems, increasingly crucial for managing complexity.

The second chapter presents a bibliometric analysis of the relationship between corporate governance and sustainability. Following the good practices by literature, an initial analysis of the contributions on the topic is carried out and then a more specific analysis of the last 5 years is carried out, a period in which there has been an exponential increase in scientific publications on the topic.

The third chapter provides an overview of the European regulation on sustainability and with specific reference to the Corporate Sustainability Due Diligence proposal, the first provision in favor of Sustainable Corporate Governance. The chapter ends with a comment by the author on the proposal currently under discussion in the European Parliament.

The fourth chapter investigates the human rights due diligence practices of European companies. In particular, through the use of mixed methodologies, a mapping of the human rights due diligence in European Public Interest Entities is carried out. In the face of a low diffusion among large European companies of due diligence practices, some governance mechanisms are identified which can be an incentive to adopt systems for the protection of human rights. The results show how the presence of a CSR Committee and the separation of offices between the chairman of the board and the CEO are some mechanisms that can be decisive especially in the light of the proposed Due Diligence Directive.

Rome, Italy Salvatore Principale

Contents

Abbreviations

COSO	Committee of Sponsoring Organizations of the Treadway Commission
CSR	Corporate Social Responsibility
CSRD	Corporate Sustainability Reporting Directive
EFRAG	European Financial Reporting Advisory Group
ESG	Environmental, Social, and Governance
EU	European
IIA	Institute of Internal Audit
NFRD	Non-financial Reporting Directive
OECD	Organisation for Economic Co-operation and Development
PIEs	Public Interest Entities

Chapter 1
Corporate Governance and Strategic Management

Keywords Corporate governance · Strategic management · Control system · Corporate governance model · Governance theories

1.1 Introduction

Corporate governance represents a theme that has fueled the debate of national and international scholars in recent years as well as has seen the regulatory intervention of regulators in different contexts (Bianco & Casavola, 1996; Melis, 2000; Zattoni & Van Ees, 2012). The attention to this issue was dictated by the centrality of governance within the corporate system.

The company is in fact defined as a complex system made up of different coordinated elements (Coase, 1937; Zappa, 1957; Onida, 1971; Bertini, 1990; Cassandro, 1992; Zanda, 2015). The company is also an open system due to the relationships and exchanges of resources it maintains with the players in the external and dynamic environment (Amaduzzi, 1969; Onida, 1971; Paoloni & Paoloni, 2021). Although companies have purposes and functions in common, they differ from each other based on the governance process and how the different elements that compose them are organized and amalgamated (Bertini, 1995; Galeotti & Garzella, 2013). Corporate choices define the company in the context in which it operates and are crucial for the achievement of its institutional goals (Caramiello, 1971; Eminente, 1986). The results deriving from strategic decisions are measured through internal-external control systems (Castellano, 2003; Mancini, 2010; Capurro et al., 2020). The results are presented and communicated to the stakeholders within the main corporate document: the financial statements (Onida, 1954; Capaldo, 1998; Quagli, 2001; Guatri, 1996).

To achieve corporate success, the company must adopt a structure (resources, activities, organizational structure, and governance system) suitable for managing and governing environmental complexity. The increased riskiness of the choices that the company has to make daily has required the use of specialist knowledge. Thus, new entities were introduced into the corporate complex which modified the corporate governance structure.

S. Principale, *Fostering Sustainability in Corporate Governance*, SIDREA Series in Accounting and Business Administration,
https://doi.org/10.1007/978-3-031-30354-8_1

The term corporate governance identifies those tools functional to the performance of strategic management. The top management is responsible for defining the strategic lines and directing corporate behavior. The purpose of corporate governance is to harmonize the relationships between the company and its interlocutors (Bertini, 2017). Strategic management activity is expressed in the definition of objectives that are in line with the plurality of perspectives of the various actors (Coda, 1989; Marchi, 2019). When the various actors of strategic management are involved and act in an organic body, corporate governance manages to satisfy the expectations of shareholders, stakeholders, and the company.

Over the years, several scholars have analyzed the phenomenon in the search for the reasons that led to the development of corporate governance. The advent of modern economies has exalted big business. The need to acquire adequate capital to meet the financial needs necessary for the new needs of business management has prompted entrepreneurs to associate themselves with other financing partners (owner capitalists). As a result, a new figure of entrepreneur has been established such as the saver or speculator shareholder, unwilling to manage the business but interested exclusively in achieving positive results to remunerate the investment made. The consequence of this is the separation of ownership and control. Other causes identified in the literature have been associated with this:

- Important privatization processes that have taken place in various states
- Fragmentation of capital
- Corporate scandals

However, it is not possible to maintain that there is a single definition in the literature. The literature on corporate governance is as large and varied as the definitions it contains. The variety of definitions is also caused by the different theoretical frameworks to which reference is made.

Here are some definitions that are commonly used in the literature:

- "A virtuous system of governance—with the agreements that inspire it, the ideas that fuel it, the models that inform it and the decisions that follow—which considers the interests of the company in a very broad context and to improve conditions of existence and manifestations of life of the socio-economic system" (Bertini, 2017).
- "Set of legal and technical institutions and rules, aimed at creating a government that is not only effective and efficient, but also correct, to protect the shareholders and all the subjects interested in the life of the company" (Consiglio Nazionale dell'Ordine dei Commercialisti, 1998, p. 5).
- "The governance role is not concerned with the running of the company, per se, but with giving overall direction to the enterprise, overseeing and controlling the executive actions of management and with satisfying legitimate expectations of accountability and regulation by interests beyond the corporate boundaries." (Tricker, 1984)
- "the system by which companies are directed and controlled" (Cadbury Report, 2.5).

- Corporate governance is investors, to a large extent, a set of mechanisms through which outsiders protect themselves against expropriation by the insiders (Eells, 1960).
- "a set of relationships between a company's management, its board, its shareholders and other stakeholders" (OECD, 2015).

1.2 Research Theories

Among the aforementioned reasons, the separation between ownership and management can be counted as the main assumption that has developed the debate on corporate governance. Thus, various theories have been developed that can be differentiated according to a different vision of the company. It is possible to define two company visions:

- Traditional view. Only the shareholders with the Board of Directors as the sole body in charge of governance are deserving of interest.
- The broader vision of corporate governance within which it is *believed* that corporate governance must be managed and oriented towards satisfying the needs of stakeholders.

From the first or second conceptualization, theories have branched out, some of which are covered below in Table 1.1.

1.2.1 Managerial Theory

Within the first strand of research it is possible to include the managerial theory which has its theoretical foundations on the model of "objective rationality." The model defines the characteristics of the "economic man" as the one who, in the absence of information asymmetries, chooses among the possible alternatives the one that produces the maximum utility. In the wake of managerial theory, various models of marginalist orientation have developed. Among the main exponents of these models are Baumol (1962) and Williamson (1967). These authors emphasize

Table 1.1 Research theories

Theory	Reference
Managerial theory	Baumol (1962)
Agency theory	Jensen and Meckling (1976)
Stakeholder theory	Freeman (1984)
Resource based view	Rumelt (1984), Wernerfelt (1995)
Stewardship view	Donaldson and Davis (1991)
Socio-emotional wealth	Gomez-Mejia et al. (2011), Berrone et al. (2012)

the dominant role of management by outlining objectives and behaviors that qualify them.

The objective of management is the dimensional growth of the company so that from the positive economic-financial and patrimonial results it can increase its usefulness. Therefore, a source of interest for management is the maximization of sales revenues. The larger the company size, the greater the positive externalities for management in terms of salary or prestige. On the other hand, a company that has a decrease in turnover, proportionally also has a loss of power about the other players in the economic system as well as a loss of trust in the subjects with whom it has established relationships.

However, the maximization of sales revenue is subject to the profit constraint. The authors argue that management considers profits as a constraint as it is necessary to maintain stable relationships with shareholders and investors. Williamson also argues that because of these different perspectives what are defined as "residual" are generated loss (Williamson, 1967). They are the higher cost component incurred by the firm due to the choices of managers who decide to allocate resources to activities that positively affect their utility function.

1.2.2 Agency Theory

The Anglo-Saxon theory of the agency, formulated for the first time by Jensen and Meckling in 1976, also derives from the separation between ownership and control. According to the approach of the authors, the company is seen as a functional means for establishing a series of contractual relationships between different actors. They have theorized the conflictual relationship between managers, those who manage the company, and the shareholders or the entrepreneur, those who are the owners. The agency theory is based on the definition of the agency relationship which means the contract between two parties: the principal and the agent. The latter undertakes to perform services on behalf of the principal. The agent is therefore delegated part of the principal's authority according to a fiduciary relationship with the task of identifying and pursuing strategic objectives.

The agent's interest, however, diverges from that of the property. The first has an interest in increasing his salary as much as possible, the second has to maximize the return on equity. By the different utility curves, the former obtains greater well-being by maximizing sales revenues, and the latter by maximizing profits (Baumol, 1962).

Consequently, the actions of the manager (agent) could be oriented towards the pursuit of his own objectives. The information asymmetries that exist between the two parties create difficulties that have repercussions on the relationship between the two actors.

Scholars have tried to fully understand the case to understand how to induce agents to align their behaviors and objectives according to the interests of the owners. To reduce the moral hazards of the agents, costs are generated for the organization (agency costs) to discourage the opportunistic behavior of the managers (Mallin et al., 2015).

The agency's problems reside in the impossibility of being able to construct a contract that provides for conditions or clauses that govern every action that the agent could undertake.

Within the agency costs, the following can be distinguished:

- Monitoring costs, costs incurred by the principal to monitor the actions taken by the manager.
- Boarding, which includes the costs incurred by agents to disclose more information to shareholders.
- Residual loss, the negative difference obtained for the optimal level despite the mitigation of monitoring and boarding costs caused by the different interests of the two actors.

Here it is useful to underline how agency problems can differ from one company to another and between different sectors and therefore the mechanisms for controlling the relationship between the parties can be heterogeneous and diverge from case to case.

In general, the theorized solution for agency costs refers to the financial markets as the only tool to identify and mitigate the alleged costs.

1.2.3 Stakeholder Theory

In 1984, Freeman defined stakeholders as any individual or group that can be influenced by the company's actions or that can influence the company's performance (Freeman, 1984, 1999; Freeman et al., 2010) This classification includes all those internal and external to the company:

- Shareholders
- Employees
- Financial institutions
- Providers
- Competitors
- Various associations
- Other

According to a broader vision of the company, the stakeholder theory emphasizes the importance of those subjects who directly or indirectly come into contact with the organization. By widening the boundaries of the company, they are therefore not seen as entities or groups external to the company but are an active part directly involved in the company's goals. On the other hand, the stakeholders are able to contribute resources in various ways directly or implicitly through bi-directional relationships that are established with the corporate complex.

By interacting with the external environment, the company should therefore also take into consideration the interests of the various parties when formulating short- and medium-long-term strategies and objectives. Therefore, when defining strategies, the company's governing body must not only consider the interests of those who hold the "shares" but also of a broad category of subjects. Having to respond also to subjects who do not hold ownership of the company, the company is encouraged to carry out socially responsible actions. However, this will be the subject of more analysis in the next chapter.

1.2.4 Resource Dependency View

This theory focuses on the role played by the board of directors (Davis & Cobb, 2010; Rumelt, 1984). From this perspective, the management body is a functional element for the company to access the resources necessary to allow the organization to continue to produce value over time. The board of directors is therefore the body capable of linking the company to the significant resources useful for allowing the company to continue over time. From another point of view, the establishment of a board of directors can be a tool of ownership to respond to challenges from the external environment and to give a signal of the attention shown by the company to the external environment (Davis & Cobb, 2010). The environment, with which the company interacts and in which the company operates and is dependent on it, is increasingly characterized by profound uncertainties and changing dynamics that can compromise the normal continuation of corporate life (Nicholson & Kiel, 2007; Wan Nicholson & Kiel, 2007; Wan Yusoff, 2012). The theory of resource dependence identifies the board of directors as the key resource for reducing the uncertainties deriving from the external environment (Pfeffer & Salancik, 1978). Therefore, directors with a high level of connections with the outside have a positive impact on company performance. They guarantee access to critical resources in relational, network, information, and capital terms. The various advantages include the contribution of qualified resources in terms of skills in the various strategic areas or better communication between the company and the various players in the economic system (Drees & Heugens, 2013).

1.2.5 Stewardship Theory

The stewardship view is a theory that takes a different position from the agency theory perspective. Unlike the latter, it has its theoretical roots in sociological and psychological fields (Donaldson & Davis, 1994). In particular, according to the theoretical system of stewardship view, a conflict of interest does not arise between the principal and agent, since the agent is interested in maximizing his own well-being which leads him to improve company performance, thus meeting the interests

Table 1.2 Agency vs stewardship

	Agency view	Stewardship view
Theory	Economics	Physicological and sociological
Manager motivators	Financial (material, external)	Non-financial (internal)
CEO duality	Yes, the president is to protect the shareholders	No, overlapping is preferred
Relationship	Conflict of interest	Aligned interests

of the shareholders and the various stakeholders (Nicholson & Kiel, 2007). In this perspective, agency costs are minimized and managers act to bring the greatest benefits to the company so that their personal advantages can be produced.

Contrary to the more classic theory, this vision highlights the alignment of the interests of ownership and management. Therefore, rather than investigating the solutions to the problems caused by the conflict of interest between the parties, the focus shifts to the definition of the tasks to be entrusted to managers to increase corporate efficiency.

The theory assumes that at the time of appointment, the interests of managers and shares agree. The cardinal principle underlying the stewardship theory is trust, which is opposed to the individualism theorized from the perspective of agency costs (Keay, 2017). Some argue that in this perspective, directors put the company's interests before their own (Schillemans & Busuioc, 2015). They are not only interested in financial compensation but find satisfaction in obtaining company results and successes. From this it follows that their motivation is also driven by dynamics that go beyond mere economic value. Similarly to the stakeholder theory, they also find satisfaction in non-financial dynamics.

Below, Table 1.2 shows some differences between the vision of the Agency and stewardship, assuming theory, manager's motivation, CEO Duality, and relationship.

1.2.6 Socio-emotional Wealth

A theory has recently been developed which has found much use, especially in studies of family businesses. Differently from the other approaches presented in the previous paragraphs, the novelty of this theory is to assume that the property is interested not only for economic purposes. The socio-emotional theory theorizes that ownership is also sensitive to issues other than the achievement of economic-financial equilibrium in the company. The major exponents of this theory have introduced the concept of "socio-emotional wealth," as the main motivation driving ownership behaviors (Gómez-Mejía et al., 2007; Berrone et al., 2010; Gomez-Mejia et al., 2011). According to these authors, they argue that in family businesses there is almost a personification of the family in the business. Berrone (2012) identifies five dimensions of socio-emotional wealth:

1. Family control and influence: family members directly or indirectly control strategic decisions and this can vary between companies depending on the authority of family members.
2. Identification of family members with the firm: the identity of the family is not distinct from that of the company but the latter is an extension of it.
3. Binding social ties: social ties are not only between family members but also extend to the other subjects with whom they come into contact and with whom they relate, from employees to the community in general.
4. Emotional attachment: the creation of a system of emotional attachments that can influence the decision-making process.
5. Renewal of family bonds to the firm through dynamic succession: one of the main objectives of the owners is to hand down the company and family values to future generations.

These dimensions are the factors that push the family to evaluate strategic choices beyond the mere achievement of maximizing profits. The owners have an interest in ensuring that the company continues to last over time and that it can be handed down to future generations and to create greater socio-emotional value. Based on these statements, several studies have suggested that the deep bond of family businesses with the territory and with the system of relationships developed over time with the various stakeholders are among the reasons that justify socially responsible behaviors of family businesses (Venturelli et al., 2020).

1.3 The Governance Model

The corporate governance models adopted by companies are different from country to country due to several factors. The causes are varied and can derive from the history, culture, and historical moment that have characterized the specific context and have given rise to peculiarities that differentiate it from other contexts that are also close to it. The doctrine aims to identify two main causes that have influenced the different governance models (Coffee Jr., 1999; La Porta et al., 2000; Denis & McConnell, 2003; Licht et al., 2005; Zattoni & Cuomo, 2008). The first cause is the legal system. In the literature, it is customary to make the difference between the system of Civil Law and that of the Common Law. The first is characterized by an important written normative fabric of the Latin matrix (Roman law). On the contrary, in the second system there is a reduced recourse to written rules in favor of a system based on the interpretation of previous jurisprudence rulings and customs.

The two legal systems have produced different implications, among which the different approach to property stands out.

The Civil law system assumes that property is an absolute right of the individual, a right over the thing. In common law system, the property is not a juridical relationship between a person and a thing but concerns the utilities that can arise from the good. This difference also spreads to the conceptualization of the company where in the Common Law system the company has a value while in the Civil system Law there is an identification between owners and the company itself.

The second motivation, which is also influenced by the previous one, concerns the financial system. Contexts that are distinguished by a particularly developed financial system that facilitates the allocation of ownership shares present a greater diffusion of ownership among the public, typical of the public company. In these contexts, a high degree of investor protection guaranteed by market surveillance bodies and the legal system can also be found. The high protection of investors, including minority shareholders together with the low degree of concentration of ownership has made corporate governance systems more efficient.

Differently, other contexts, characterized by a lesser development of the financed market, have encouraged the financing of entrepreneurial activities mainly from the banking system headed by the same applicant company. In the face of a low concentration, the control assumes a high relevance.

1.3.1 UK Model

The doctrine associates the English model with the US one due to the similar characteristics of the two contexts. Both are characterized by a large market and by the presence of medium and large companies with a low concentration of ownership in favor of a high fragmentation of ownership (Trequattrini, 1999). The US context is characterized by a greater degree of fragmentation than the British one.

Although Great Britain has a high degree of presence of public companies, it should be noted that even in this context it experienced early family capitalism. This phase was overcome after the beginning of the twentieth century and even more in the ‘80s of the same century due to profound privatization processes which reduced the concentration of ownership of British companies and introduced institutional investors into the economic system stably, such as pension funds or investment funds (venture capital). The presence of these investors who are less interested in the typical management practices of the company than in the realization of proceeds against future sales has required the presence of top management with broad management roles to ensure company development scenarios in the medium-long term.

The ease of reallocating ownership was also facilitated by the presence in various capacities of some private actors such as accounting houses or commercial banks. With a view to a high guarantee of the investor, the former has the purpose of guaranteeing the truthfulness and correctness of the accounting data. Commercial banks have contributed to improving the system by supporting, for example, companies through their activity in listing on regulated markets.

Corporate governance has been regulated since 1985 by the Companies Act, subsequently updated in 1985 and 2006 (Pletz & Upson, 2019). The English model is characterized by being one-tier system in which the administrative body is the board of directors which is made up of executive and non-executive directors. Management power is delegated to the executive directors while the latter have a supervisory role. The board also has the task of appointing the chairman, a position that can also be held by the CEO. For listed companies, the UK Corporate Governance Code was introduced in 2019.

1.3.2 German Model

Two elements characterize the German model: the role of the banking system and the protection of stakeholders. The cooperative relationship established over the years between German industry and the banking system has been useful for accelerating the growth process of the German economy. The phenomena of undercapitalization were very frequent in the face of extensive recourse to bank debt. In recent years, the German system has tried to open up to the financial markets as evidenced by the thickness and importance assumed in the European context by the Frankfurt Stock Exchange (Goncharov et al., 2006; Lane, 2016).

Despite the development of international markets and the intervention of the national legislator (for example with the creation of a secondary market), the role of German banks in companies has remained of the first order. In fact, over the years the banks have accumulated several share packages of German companies. In fact, German banks influence company management by directly owning shares of companies with voting rights and by inserting their representatives in the governing bodies.

On the other hand, the German system seeks to guarantee the protection of stakeholders. The success and creation of corporate value in the medium to long term cannot be separated from corporate management also oriented towards the satisfaction of the stakeholders. German companies are therefore oriented towards implementing a corporate culture aimed at respecting various stakeholders and in compliance with ethical principles. In addition to this, concrete tools are envisaged to protect the various stakeholders, such as employees. The latter are provided with the tools for active participation in the top corporate levels. In particular, they are represented within the control body and the establishment of a body (Betriebsrat is also envisaged, which can express its thoughts regarding the activities or problems relating to personnel).

The Supervisory Board is the body set up to protect the interests of the various stakeholders. The two-tiered system has been present in Germany since 1870 which provides for the Management Board with roles of administration and management of the company supported by the Supervisory Board which appoints the members (Chhillar & Lellapalli, 2015).

1.3.3 *The Italian System*

The Italian context was characterized by a strong undercapitalization of the industrial fabric (Trequattrini, 1999) caused by various factors. Among these we highlight the widespread presence of family-run businesses and the strong presence of the State in various productive sectors. This was associated with the development of the official stock exchange and financial markets only towards the end of the century. Banks have only played and maintained the role of financial intermediaries and have not given the push to overcome the purely familiar setting of Italian entrepreneurship (Melis & Zattoni, 2017).

However, there has been a change in the *status quo* since the 1990s. Global changes, globalization, and technological and IT innovation have prompted the Italian legislator to reflections that have led him to intervene to stimulate a change to encourage the growth of the Italian entrepreneurial fabric made up of a high presence of small and medium-sized businesses. The legislator has intervened in the financial system so that it follows the expansive examples that took place in advance in other contexts and other member countries. Among the various interventions, the Consolidated Act introduced by Legislative Decree no. 58 of 1998 represented a milestone as it introduced elements of modernity in the panorama of financial intermediation and also important implications in corporate governance. On this last point, in this period also in Italy importance is beginning to be attributed to corporate governance and the protection of minority shareholders. Subsequent regulatory interventions have further increased the importance of these two factors in conjunction with an intensification of the internal and external control systems and of the reporting systems.

Finally, since 2003, listed companies have been able to independently decide the governance system they want to adopt, distinguishing between: ordinary, dualistic, and monistic. The first model (art. 2380 of the civil code) provides for the presence of the board of directors with management roles and the board of statutory auditors with control and supervisory functions. Based on the German model, the second model (art. 2409 octies of the civil code) prepares the establishment of the management body and the supervisory board whose duties have been described in the previous paragraph. Lastly, the one-tier model (art. 2409 sexiesdecies of the Italian Civil Code) merges the functions of administration and control into a single body, although a control committee is nominated within the board of directors.

1.4 Control Systems

The control functions have been and are the subject of strong attention among practitioners and academics. The financial crisis of 2007–2009 and various industrial scandals gave impetus to a lively discussion that questioned the effectiveness of company control systems and confirmed the importance of implementing a control system that is up to date with growing challenges affecting the company (D'Onza, 2008; Marchi, 2020).

According to this approach, the corporate boards have the task of controlling and supervising the risks to which the company is exposed so that they do not produce negative effects on the creation of corporate value (Brown et al., 2009; Allegrini & D'Onza, 2011).

Control systems can be internal or external to the company system. All those actors who are outside the corporate scope fall within external control, which mainly affects listed companies. The various actors exercise control over the information disclosed by companies to protect the various categories of stakeholders and discourage non-transparent behavior by companies.

The external control systems vary from country to country but in general they fall within this category:

- Market Authority
- External Audit
- Tax Authority
- Judicial Authorities
- Various public entities

Conversely, internal controls pertain to control systems that the company must adopt internally. A control system definition was given by Committee of Sponsoring Organizations of the Treadway Commission (COSO), an organization that has defined one of the approaches and reference frameworks for risk management to better guide corporate strategies. The internal control system was defined as "a process, effected by an entity's board of directors, management, and other personnel, designed to provide reasonable assurance regarding the achievement of objectives relating to operations, reporting, and compliance."

In order for an effective control system to be implemented, the corporate bodies should tend to:

1. Achieve its strategic objectives
2. Provide reliable financial reporting to internal and external stakeholders
3. Operate its business efficiently and effectively
4. Comply with all applicable laws and regulations
5. Safeguard its assets
6. Specifies suitable objectives
7. Identifies and analyzes risk
8. Assesses fraud risk
9. Identifies and analyzes significant change
10. Selects and develops control activities
11. Selects and develops general controls over technology
12. Deploys control activities through policies and procedures
13. Uses relevant information
14. Communicates internally
15. Communicates externally

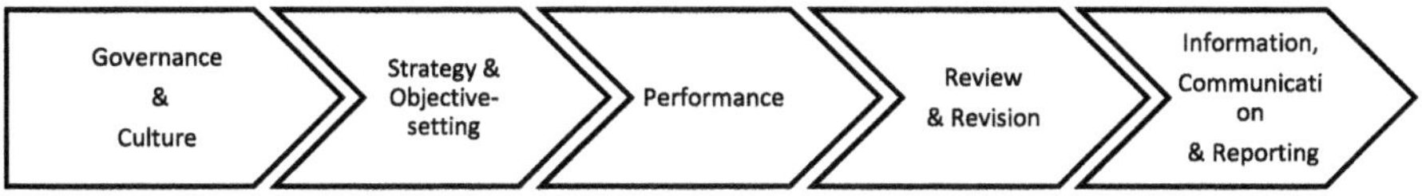

Fig. 1.1 COSO framework

16. Conducts ongoing and/or separate evaluations
17. Evaluates and communicate deficiencies

The internal systems refer to the various corporate governance bodies:

- Board of directors
- Independent directors
- Board of statutory auditors
- Internal audits
- Internal committees
- Risk management

These bodies have the aim of ensuring that the company achieves the pre-established objectives and results. Among these, growing importance is taking on the function of internal audit and risk management.

The internal audit plays a role of management consultant by making documented and informed criticisms of the processes that pertain to governance and risk management. Being an independent body free from influences, the internal audit carries out activities of supervision and inspection of the processes in order to have an in-depth knowledge of the corporate processes. In addition, the forward-thinking internal audit function also attempts to inform management of frontier challenges before they become real risks to the company. The Institute of Internal Audit (IIA) highlights that if internal audit acts objectively and responsibly, it can provide greater value to the company by providing consultancy services oriented towards continuous process improvement.

Regarding risk management, it is a function that has become a critical function of corporate governance following recent corporate failures, not least the recent pandemic crisis. This function, required of listed companies, is therefore necessary for companies to implement and define effective procedures that regulate corporate risk management activities. For this reason, the COSO suggests that it does not concern only one company function but rather must be rooted in all levels of the company. COSO does not define enterprise risk management as a process but of "the culture, capabilities, and practices that organizations integrate with strategy-setting and apply when they carry out that strategy, to manage risk in creating, preserving, and realizing value" (Committee of Sponsoring Oganizations of the Treadway Commission, 2017).

The latest version of the framework identifies five components and 20 goals (Fig. 1.1).

The presence of the five categories highlights how much risk management is not to be considered as a separate activity but integrated into corporate strategies. In fact, the board determines the strategies and risk profiles to be assumed as well as disseminates the culture in the various underlying levels. In addition, in their leadership role, directors must oversee that management pays due attention to risks and that appropriate measures are taken to mitigate them. However, the personnel of the company as a whole are responsible for implementing risk management and mitigation policies. Once the degree of risk acceptance has been defined, the risk management process is divided into:

- Risk Identification
- Risk Assessment
- Risk Treatment
- Risk Monitoring and Reporting

References

Allegrini, M., & D'Onza, G. (2011). Corporate governance, risk management e responsabilità sociale fra presente e futuro dell'attività di internal auditing. *Management Control, 2011*(1), 151–178.

Amaduzzi, A. (1969). *L'azienda nel suo sistema e nell'ordine delle sue rilevazioni.* Unione Tipografico-Editrice Torinese.

Baumol, W. (1962). On the theory of expansion of the firm. *The American Economic Review, 52*(5), 1078–1087.

Berrone, P., Cruz, C., Gomez-Mejia, L. R., & Larraza-Kintana, M. (2010). Socioemotional wealth and corporate responses to institutional pressures: Do family-controlled firms pollute less? *Administrative Science Quarterly, 55*(1), 82–113.

Berrone, P., Cruz, C., & Gomez-Mejia, L. R. (2012). Socioemotional wealth in family firms. *Family Business Review, 25*(3), 258–279.

Bertini, U. (1990). *Il sistema d'azienda : schema di analisi. In Studi di economia e politica aziendale*. Giappichelli.

Bertini, U. (1995). Scritti di politica aziendale. In *Studi di economia e politica aziendale.* Giappichelli.

Bertini, U. (2017). La corporate governance, fattore di superamento della crisi e di sviluppo dell'economia. *RIREA, 1*, 14–20.

Bianco, M., & Casavola, P. (1996). Corporate governance in Italia: alcuni fatti e problemi aperti. *Rivista delle società, 41*(2–3), 426–439.

Brown, I., Steen, A., & Foreman, J. (2009). Risk management in corporate governance: A review and proposal. *Corporate Governance: An International Review, 17*(5), 546–558.

Cadbury, A. (1992). *Report of the committee on the financial aspects of corporate governance*. Gee & Co.

Capaldo, P. (1998). *Reddito, capitale e bilancio di esercizio: un'introduzione*. Giuffrè.

Capurro, R., Morrone, C., Garzella, S., & Fiorentino, R. (2020). La creazione del valore: il necessario completamento del sistema di controllo e di comunicazione aziendale. *Management Control*, 37–55.

Caramiello, C. (1971). *Programmi e piani aziendali*. Isedi.
Cassandro, P. E. (1992). *Trattato di Ragioneria: L'economia delle aziende e il suo controllo*. Cacucci.
Castellano, N. G. (2003). *Controllo di gestione ed informazioni. Un approccio integrato*. Giuffrè.
Chhillar, P., & Lellapalli, R. V. (2015). Divergence or convergence: Paradoxes in corporate governance? *Corporate Governance*.
Coase, R. H. (1937). The nature of the firm. *Economica, 4*(16), 386–405.
Coda, V. (1989). *Orientamento strategico dell'impresa*. Utet.
Coffee, J. C., Jr. (1999). Privatization and corporate governance: The lessons from securities market failure. *SSRN Electronic Journal*.
Committee of Sponsoring Oganizations of the Treadway Commission. (2017). *Enterprise risk management integrating with strategy and performance*.
Consiglio Nazionale dei Dottori Commercialisti. (1998). *Aspetti generali della riforma del Corporate Governance: profili comparatistici, Supplemento a "Il Giornale dei Dottori Commercialisti"*, n. 10.
D'Onza, G. (2008). *Il sistema di controllo interno nella prospettiva del risk management* (Vol. 81). Giuffrè editore.
Davis, G. F., & Cobb, J. A. (2010). Resource dependence theory: Past and future. *Research in the Sociology of Organizations, 28*, 21.
Denis, D. K., & McConnell, J. J. (2003). International corporate governance. *Journal of Financial and Quantitative Analysis, 38*(1), 1–36.
Donaldson, L., & Davis, J. H. (1991). Stewardship theory or agency theory: CEO governance and shareholder returns. *Australian Journal of Management, 16*(1), 49–64.
Donaldson, L., & Davis, J. H. (1994). Boards and company performance – Research challenges the conventional wisdom. *Corporate Governance: An International Review, 2*(3), 151–160.
Drees, J. M., & Heugens, P. P. M. A. R. (2013). Synthesizing and extending resource dependence theory: A meta-analysis. *Journal of Management, 39*(6), 1666–1698.
Eells, R. (1960). *The meaning of modern business: An introduction to the philosophy of large corporate enterprise*. Columbia University Press.
Eminente, G. (1986). *Pianificazione e gestione strategica dell'impresa*. Il Mulino.
Freeman, R. E. (1984). *Strategic management: A stakeholder approach*. Pitman.
Freeman, R. E. (1999). Divergent stakeholder theory. *Academy of Management Review, 24*(2), 233–236.
Freeman, R. E., Harrison, J. S., Wicks, A. C., Parmar, B. L., & De Colle, S. (2010). *Stakeholder theory: The state of the art*. Cambridge University Press.
Galeotti, M., & Garzella, S. (2013). *Governo strategico dell'azienda*. Giappichelli Editore.
Gómez-Mejía, L. R., Haynes, K. T., Núñez-Nickel, M., Jacobson, K. J. L., & Moyano-Fuentes, J. (2007). Socioemotional wealth and business risks in family-controlled firms: Evidence from Spanish olive oil mills. *Administrative Science Quarterly, 52*(1), 106–137.
Gomez-Mejia, L. R., Cruz, C., Berrone, P., & de Castro, J. (2011). The bind that ties: Socioemotional wealth preservation in family firms. *Academy of Management Annals, 5*(1), 653–707.
Goncharov, I., Werner, J. R., & Zimmermann, J. (2006). Does compliance with the German corporate governance code have an impact on stock valuation? An empirical analysis. *Corporate Governance: An International Review, 14*(5), 432–445.
Guatri, L. (1996). *L'inettitudine dei risultati contabili a esprimere la performance dell'impresa. Dall'utile di bilancio al risultato economico integrato, in "La valutazione delle aziende"*, 2.
Jensen, M. C., & Meckling, W. H. (1976). Theory of the firm: Managerial behavior, agency costs and ownership structure. *Journal of Financial Economics, 3*(4), 305–360.
Keay, A. (2017). Stewardship theory: Is board accountability necessary? *International Journal of Law and Management, 59*(6), 1292–1314.

La Porta, R., Lopez-De-Silanes, F., Shleifer, A., & Vishny, R. (2000). Investor protection and corporate governance. *Journal of Financial Economics, 58*(1–2), 3–27.

Lane, C. (2016). Changes in corporate governance of German corporations: Convergence to the Anglo-American model, *7*(2–3), 79–100.

Licht, A. N., Goldschmidt, C., & Schwartz, S. H. (2005). Culture, law, and corporate governance. *International Review of Law and Economics, 25*(2), 229–255.

Mallin, C., Melis, A., & Gaia, S. (2015). The remuneration of independent directors in the UK and Italy: An empirical analysis based on agency theory. *International Business Review, 24*(2), 175–186.

Mancini, D. (2010). Le condizioni di efficacia del sistema di controllo aziendale. In *Qualità e Sicurezza del Sistema di Controllo*. Giappichelli.

Marchi, L. (2019). Governo delle aziende e creazione di valore: da una prospettiva finanziaria ad una prospettiva economico-sociale. *Management Control, 1*.

Marchi, L. (2020). Dalla crisi allo sviluppo sostenibile. Il ruolo dei sistemi di misurazione e controllo. *Management Control, 3*, 5–16.

Melis, A. (2000). Corporate governance in Italy. *Corporate Governance: An International Review, 8*(4), 347–355.

Melis, A., & Zattoni, A. (2017). *A primer on corporate governance: Italy*. Business Expert Press.

Nicholson, G. J., & Kiel, G. C. (2007). Can directors impact performance? A case-based test of three theories of corporate governance. *Corporate Governance: An International Review, 15*(4), 585–608.

OECD. (2015). *OECD principles of corporate governance*. https://www.oecd.org/daf/ca/g20-oecdprinciples-of-corporate-governance-2015-9789264236882-en.htm

Onida, P. (1954). *L'azienda: primi principî di gestione e di organizzazione*. Giuffrè.

Onida, P. (1971). *Economia d'azienda*. UTET.

Paoloni, M., & Paoloni, P. (2021). *Introduzione ed orientamento allo studio delle aziende*. Giappichelli.

Pfeffer, J., & Salancik, G. R. (1978). *The external control of organizations: A resource dependence perspective*.

Pletz, S., & Upson, J. (2019). The normative evolution of corporate governance in the UK: An empirical analysis (1995–2014). *Corporate Governance: The International Journal of Business in Society*.

Quagli, A. (2001). L'informativa volontaria nel bilancio: ruolo, modalità e recenti tendenze. *Revisione contabile, 41*.

Rumelt, R. P. (1984). Towards a strategic theory of the firm. Alternative theories of the firm. *Competitive Strategic Management*, 556–570.

Schillemans, T., & Busuioc, M. (2015). Predicting public sector accountability: From agency drift to forum drift. *Journal of Public Administration Research and Theory, 25*(1), 191–215.

Trequattrini, R. (1999). *Economia aziendale e nuovi modelli di corporate governance: esperienze a confronto*. Giappichelli.

Tricker, R. I. (1984). *Corporate governance: Practices, procedures, and powers in British companies and their boards of directors*. Gower Publishing Company.

Venturelli, A., Principale, S., Ligorio, L., & Cosma, S. (2020). Walking the talk in family firms. An empirical investigation of CSR communication and practices. *Corporate Social Responsibility and Environmental Management*. csr.2064.

Wan Yusoff, W. F. (2012). Insight of corporate governance theories. *Journal of Business and Management, 1*(1), 52–63.

Wernerfelt, B. (1995). The resource-based view of the firm: Ten years after. *Strategic Management Journal, 16*(3), 171–174.

Williamson, O. E. (1967). *The economics of discretionary behavior: Managerial objectives in a theory of the firm*. Markham Publishing Company.

Zanda, G. (2015). *Fondamenti di economia aziendale*. Giappichelli.

Zappa, G. (1957). *Le produzioni nell'economia delle imprese*. Giuffré.

Zattoni, A., & Cuomo, F. (2008). Why adopt codes of good governance? A comparison of institutional and efficiency perspectives. *Corporate Governance: An International Review, 16*(1), 1–15.

Zattoni, A., & Van Ees, H. (2012). How to contribute to the development of a global understanding of corporate governance? Reflections from submitted and published articles in CGIR. *Corporate Governance: An International Review, 20*(1), 106–118.

Chapter 2
Corporate Governance and Sustainability

Keywords Corporate social responsibility · Sustainable corporate governance · Accountability · CSR committee · Bibliometric analysis

2.1 Introduction

Over the years the vision of the company has been consolidated as a role of the company in society (Bertini, 1995; Castellani, 2015; Lombardi, 2021). All companies (public and private, profit or non-profit) should pursue long-term economic equilibrium and the satisfaction of human needs (Marchi, 2019; Ricci et al., 2020). This was associated with the awareness that traditional models of value creation should be associated and integrated with elements that consider the increase in collective well-being (Adams, 2017).

The conceptualization of Corporate Social Responsibility (CSR) dates back to the seventies when, in the context of the United States of America, a debate associated with business ethics began. It is in this context that the stakeholder theory was developed (Freeman, 1984) which served as a theoretical justification for firms to formulate corporate strategies also in consideration of the social implications for the categories of stakeholders.

Subsequently, CSR has been the subject of discussion by various scholars up to the present day (Garzella, 2018; Mancini et al., 2016).

Since CSR pertains to company management, companies are called to incorporate the requests of the various stakeholders into their strategies. Given the above, the crucial importance of corporate governance is affirmed since it defines the policies and strategies that can combine, on the one hand, the remuneration of all corporate subjects and, on the other, guarantee economic and sustainable growth of the economy (Di Cagno et al., 2019). Strategic management as already specified in the previous chapter, must consider the expectations of both shareholders and stakeholders in planning strategic choices (Galeotti, 2006). Some of the main scholars of business administration (Coronella et al., 2018) already in the second part of the last millennium theorized that a well-governed company is capable of becoming a means

S. Principale, *Fostering Sustainability in Corporate Governance*, SIDREA Series in Accounting and Business Administration,
https://doi.org/10.1007/978-3-031-30354-8_2

of guaranteeing and increasing social well-being also subject to the principle of the economy (Onida, 1971).

Furthermore, the prejudice against CSR, which was seen as a cost that could negatively affect the company's economic equilibrium, seems to have been overcome recently. Today there is greater awareness of the phenomenon by seeing CSR as an opportunity rather than a cost (Ricci et al., 2020; Capurro et al., 2020). International literature has shown how the benefits of socially responsible behavior outweigh the costs related to the implementation of systems that favor sustainable practices (increased operating and financing costs, measurement costs, and organizational costs).

The attention paid to the company–environment relationship as well as the relevance of the expectations of the various stakeholders has also led to changes in corporate communication. Virtuous examples of companies that voluntarily communicated information relating to the environmental, social, and governance (ESG) fields have increased exponentially to satisfy the needs of stakeholders (De Villiers & Marques, 2016; Rezaee & Tuo, 2017; Rossi et al., 2021). Moreover, after an initial period in which the topic was the prerogative of a few, in recent years the topic has exploded, arriving to be discussed by international organizations and policymakers. National and international regulators are increasingly implementing policies to raise corporate awareness of ESG issues and the Sustainable Development Goals (SDGs). Countries around the world are committed to achieving some ambitious goals by 2030 so as not to jeopardize the future of future generations. Academics and organizations believe that the involvement of businesses is necessary for the achievement of the objectives of the 2030 Agenda.

2.2 Theories

As the theme of CSR has matured, different theories regarding the relationship between corporate governance and sustainability have also developed and perfected (Elmaghrabi, 2021). The following table summarizes some of the theories most commonly used by scholars in the literature (Table 2.1).

As discussed in the previous chapter, the agency theory entrusts corporate governance to align the objectives of managers with those of shareholders. Agency

Table 2.1 Theories

Theory	Explanation
Agency theory	Integration of CSR into the strategy serves as a control tool
Stakeholder theory	Governance considers stakeholder requests by adopting CSR practices and communication
Resource dependence theory	CSR is a useful resource for obtaining competitive advantage.
Legitimacy theory	Tool to legitimize the company towards the community

theory theorists argue that managers have the incentive to invest resources in CSR if they are functional to increase reputation towards citizens and stakeholders (McWilliams & Siegel, 2001; Jain & Jamali, 2016). In this perspective, CSR is seen as a cost associated with the company. He argued that managers use CSR to promote their programs and careers to the detriment of shareholders. However, others argue that CSR investing could reduce agency costs since it would reduce conflicts between stocks and investors. Like governance mechanisms, voluntary disclosure is also a means used by shareholders to supervise and control the work of managers (Garcia Sanchez et al., 2011; De Villiers & Hsiao, 2018). For the company, all stakeholders are equally important and it is responsible for acting in their interests (Freeman et al., 2010).

Scholars who have studied the phenomenon under the theoretical framework of the legitimacy theory argue that the corporate volitional body decides to formulate sustainability-oriented strategies to legitimize itself in the eyes of the stakeholders. The legitimacy theory argues that society cannot exist unless considered within the social context (Guthrie & Parker, 1989). The company cannot survive in the medium-long term if it does not operate according to a system of values recognized by the society in which it operates. Therefore, companies adopt responsible behavior to maintain a link with society and to be able to continue to operate in that context. CSR practices and disclosure are part of corporate strategies to legitimize themselves so that society recognizes that the company has a system of values (Deegan et al., 2002; Deegan, 2019).

The stakeholder theory has as its cornerstone a broader vision of the company that extends its boundaries by also incorporating the subjects with whom it enters into direct and indirect relationships. In this sense, companies invest resources in socially responsible activities since the corporate purpose does not only include the generation of profits and durability over time but also social and ethical purposes (Carroll, 1991). According to this view, when defining corporate strategies, managers must take into account the interests of the various categories of stakeholders as much as their own and those of the shareholders (growth, stability, etc.) (Donaldson & Preston, 1995).

2.3 Methodology

For a comprehensive analysis of the studies on the subject, following the most recent bibliometric analysis practices (Caputo et al., 2018; Belloque et al., 2021), a literature review was added to the bibliometric analysis. The comparative approach of both methodologies allows for limiting the methodological risks of both methods (Bartolacci et al., 2020).

The data used in this study are extracted from the source Scopus (Mongeon & Paul-Hus, 2015). This source is one of the largest and most reliable databases for bibliometric studies (Falagas et al., 2008; Bartolacci et al., 2020). It contains a large number of publications from 1900 to date with all the bibliographic information necessary for the application of this methodology (Ye et al., 2020).

The keyword search was carried out using the following string: TS = ("CORPORATE GOVERNCANCE") AND TS = ('SUSTAINAB*' OR 'ESG' OR 'CSR' OR 'CORPORATE SOCIAL RESPONSIBILITY'). To ensure a comprehensive search of the articles, the keywords had to be presented either in the title, or in the abstract or in the keywords. Later some filters were applied. Only scientific articles in English published in journals relating to the Business, Management, and Accounting area were included (Caputo et al., 2021).

In accordance with recent best practices in bibliometry, the analysis was performed through the use of bibliometrix and VosViewer. Bibliometrix is an R package for quantitative research in bibliometry (Aria & Cuccurullo, 2017). Statistical analyses for journals and documents were carried out with the software. Instead, VosViewer was used for keywords analysis. Using this method, it is possible to investigate the contents of the selected works to determine the underlying macro-themes. Specifically, network visualization and overlay visualization were adopted. For network visualization, the elements are represented by circles of dimensions the larger the more important the element is. Furthermore, the closer the elements are to each other, the stronger their relationship is. On the other hand, through the overlay visualization it is possible to graphically view the development and temporal trend of the topics.

2.4 Corporate Governance and Sustainability

A preliminary analysis was carried out to evaluate the areas in which the relationship between governance and sustainability was investigated.

As shown in Fig. 2.1, the major contributions on the topic concerned the Business, Management, and Accounting area (1434), followed by the Social Sciences area (829) and Economics (720). It is interesting to observe how the subject matter is multidisciplinary. Contributions are also found in different areas such as Engineering (144) or psychology.

2.4.1 Corporate Governance and Sustainability in Management and Accounting Studies

Journal

The increase in the relevance of sustainability issues was subsequently accompanied by an increase in studies also relating to corporate governance. The figure shows the trend of scientific contributions on the topic over time (Fig. 2.2).

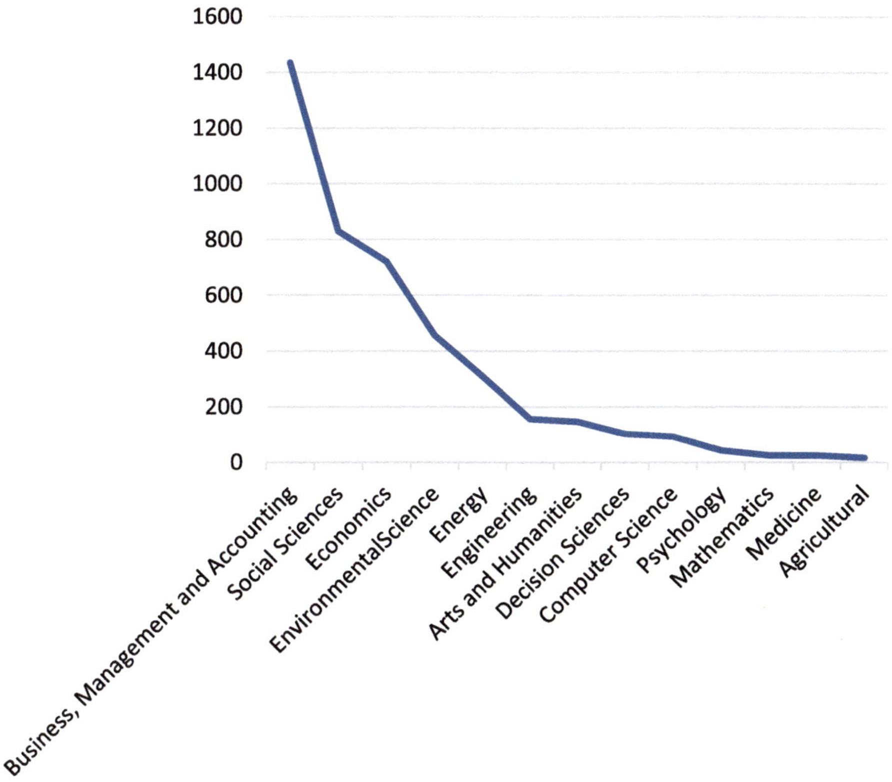

Fig. 2.1 Scientific area. Source: Author elaboration

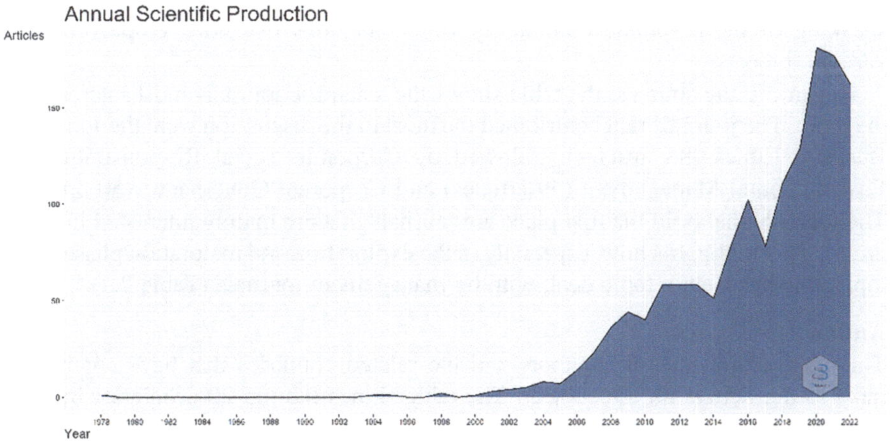

Fig. 2.2 Annual scientific production. Source: Author elaboration

Table 2.2 Most relevant sources

Sources	Articles
Journal of Business Ethics	83
Corporate Social Responsibility and Environmental Management	59
Corporate Governance (Bingley)	50
Social Responsibility Journal	48
Business Strategy and the Environment	45
Corporate Governance: An International Review	41
Journal of Cleaner Production	37
Corporate Governance	22
International Journal of Law and Management	19
Management Decision	19
Journal of Corporate Finance	18
Journal of Management and Governance	18
Sustainability Accounting Management and Policy Journal	18
Journal of Global Responsibility	16
Journal of Asian Finance Economics and Business	14
International Journal of Disclosure and Governance	13
Indian Journal of Corporate Governance	12
International Journal of Accounting and Information Management	12

The binomial governance-sustainability has been the subject of discussion by accounting scholars in the last two decades. From 2000 onwards, the curve assumed an increasing trend, reaching its peak in 2020 with 162 scientific contributions. The curve assumed an exponential trend in the years between 2017 and 2020. The first article dealing with the issues of social and environmental sustainability was published in 1978 (Halal, 1978). This work defines governance in a broad sense, speaking of the corporate community which includes investors, employees, and various subjects.

Regarding the sources, the table shows the scientific journals most interested in the topic. The journals that contributed the most to the discussion were the Journal of Business Ethics (83 articles), followed by Corporate Social Responsibility and Environmental Management (59 articles) and Corporate Governance (50 articles). The journals that hold the first place are journals that are mainly interested in ethics issues. This highlights how, especially in the exploration and maturation phase of the topic, this has been a topic dealt with by management journals (Table 2.2).

Author

This section indicates the authors and the related countries that have contributed most to the debate on the subject. The table shows the top 20 scholars who have distinguished themselves for their research on corporate governance in the wake of sustainability (Table 2.3).

Velte is the author who has produced the most studies (20) on the topic being analyzed. In addition to the author, Hussainey and Garcìa-Sanchez have also devoted much attention to the topic, the first with the publication of ten scientific

Table 2.3 Authors

Authors	Articles
Velte P	20
Hussainey K	10
García-Sánchez Im	9
Jarboui A	8
Martínez-Ferrero J	8
Zaman R	7
Gallego-Álvarez I	6
Stawinoga M	6
Young S	6
Galbreath J	5

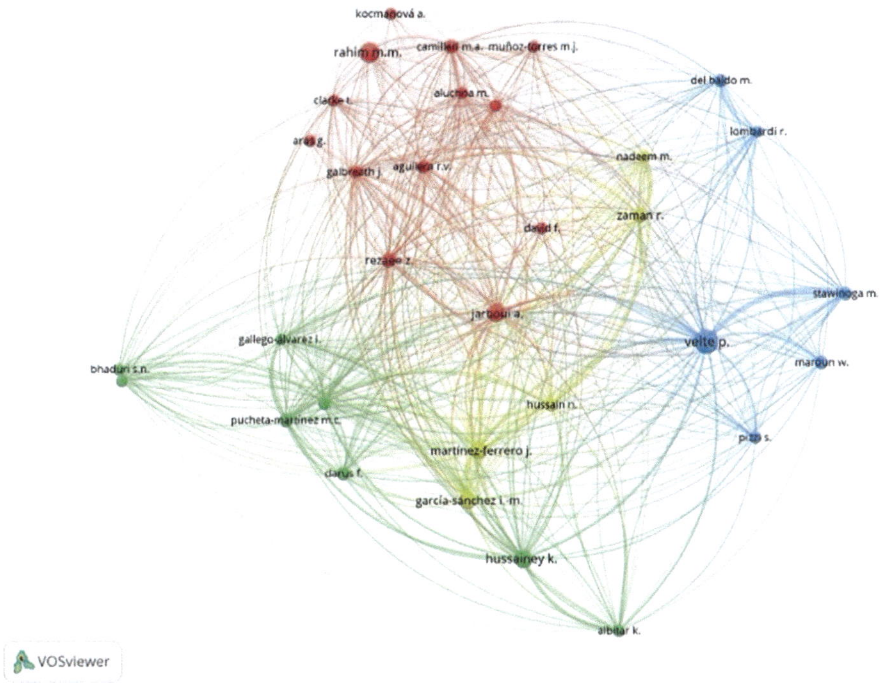

Fig. 2.3 Network analysis. Source: Author elaboration

articles and the second with nine contributions. Figure 2.3 reports the bibliographic coupling analysis. This analysis shows the relationships between the authors (Fig. 2.4).

The analysis by country, on the other hand, highlights the countries most analyzed by scholars. In particular, the most investigated countries, as can be seen from the graph, are in order:

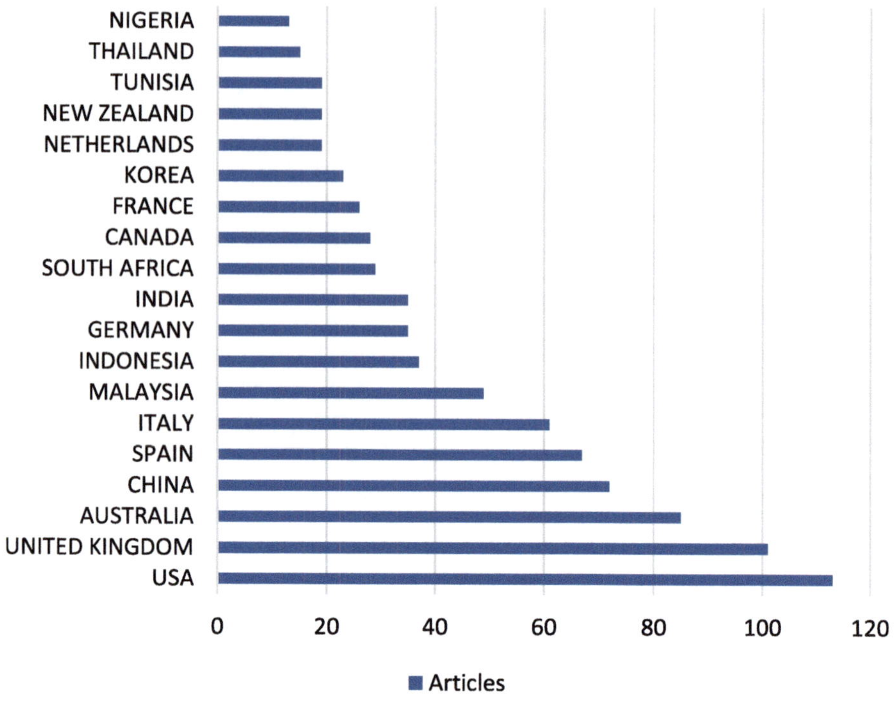

Fig. 2.4 Analysis by country. Source: Author elaboration

- USA (113 articles)
- United Kingdom (101 articles)
- Australia (85 articles)
- China (72 articles)
- Spain (67 articles)
- Italy (61 articles)

Document

The following Table 2.4 shows the contributions categorized by number of citations. The citation analysis makes it possible to highlight which works have acted as a guide for corporate governance work in recent years.

The articles that obtained the most citations were the contributions of (Barnea & Rubin, 2010; Harjoto & Jo, 2011) and of (Khan et al., 2013). These first set of articles investigated the relationship between management and socially responsible practices (Table 2.5).

Within the analysis by documents, the table above shows the results for the most cited articles within the sample and the analysis of references. The analysis of the local citations confirms what is highlighted by the first analysis. In fact, the articles that have contributed most to the development of the theme are also present in the local citations. On the other hand, the analysis of the references reveals the presence

Table 2.4 Most relevant document

Paper	Total citations	CT per year
Barnea A, 2010, J Bus Ethics	907	69.7692
Jo H, 2011, J Bus Ethics	639	53.25
Khan A, 2013, J Bus Ethics	568	56.8
Le Breton-Miller I, 2006, Entrep Theory Pract	549	32.2941
Jackson G, 2010, J Bus Ethics	495	38.0769
Jo H, 2012, J Bus Ethics	449	40.8182
Prior D, 2008, Corp Gov	443	29.5333
Harjoto MA, 2011, J Bus Ethics	437	36.4167
Michelon G, 2012, J Manage Gov	430	39.0909
Krüger P, 2015, J Financ Econ	423	52.875
Kolk A, 2008, Bus Strategy Environ	413	27.5333

of theoretical works used by scholars as a theoretical basis for the development of their research.

Occurrence analysis was conducted to analyze all the keywords present in the analyzed sample. This analysis is used to highlight the different research areas investigated by scholars with respect to the specific topic (Fig. 2.5).

The following figure highlights four different areas:

- Corporate governance theory (red cluster): corporate governance, stakeholder theory, legitimacy theory, agency theory, csr disclosure, firm performance, ownership structure, board independence, board characteristics, disclosure, Malaysia.
- Governance and sustainability (Green cluster): sustainability, governance, environmental social and governance, corporate social performance, social responsibility, corporate responsibility, environmental, performance, esg, ethics, firm value.
- Governance and reporting (Yellow cluster): board of directors, corporate sustainability, integrated reporting, sustainability reporting stakeholder engagement, gender diversity, sustainable development, sustainable development goals.
- Corporate governance and emerging economies (blu cluster): corporate social responsibility, corporate social responsibility performance, financial performance, earnings management, earnings, institutional theory, emerging markets, india, china, csr,

2.5 Recent Literature on the Topic

Since, as shown in Fig. 2.6, there has been a significant increase in scientific articles since 2017, this paragraph focuses on the last 5 years to highlight the latest research trends by classifying the sub-themes treated by scholars and emphasizing the themes mostly frontier.

Table 2.5 Local references

Cited references	Cit.	Local cited	Cit.
Jensen, MC, Meckling, WH, Theory of the firm: Managerial behavior, agency costs and ownership structure (1976) Journal of Financial Economics, 3 (4), pp. 305–360	102	Barnea A, 2010, J Bus Ethics	115
Haniffa, RM, Cooke, TE, The impact of culture and governance on corporate social reporting (2005) Journal of Accounting and Public Policy, 24 (5), pp. 391–430	61	Michelon G, 2012, J Manage Gov	107
Mcwilliams, A., Siegel, D., Corporate social responsibility: A theory of the firm perspective (2001) Academy of Management Review, 26 (1), pp. 117–127	60	Khan A, 2013, J Bus Ethics	100
Barnea, A., Rubin, A., Corporate social responsibility as a conflict between shareholders (2010) Journal of Business Ethics, 97 (1), pp. 71–86	53	Jo H, 2011, J Bus Ethics	96
Johnson, RA, Greening, DW, The effects of corporate governance and institutional ownership types on corporate social performance (1999) Academy of Management Journal, 42 (5), pp. 564–576	52	Jo H, 2012, J Bus Ethics	87
Bear, S., Rahman, N., Post, C., The impact of board diversity and gender composition on corporate social responsibility and firm reputation (2010) Journal of Business Ethics, 97 (2), pp. 207–221	48	Harjoto MA, 2011, J Bus Ethics	82
Donaldson, T., Preston, LE, The stakeholder theory of the corporation: Concepts, evidence, and implications (1995) Academy of Management Review, 20 (1), pp. 65–91	47	Said R, 2009, Soc Responsib J	75
Khan, A., Muttakin, MB, Siddiqui, J., Corporate governance and corporate social responsibility disclosures: Evidence from an emerging economy (2013) Journal of Business Ethics, 114 (2), pp. 207–223	44	Jizi MI, 2014, J Bus Ethics	71
Orlitzky, M., Schmidt, FL, Rynes, SL, Corporate social and financial performance: A meta-analysis (2003) Organization Studies, 24 (3), pp. 403–441	44	Arora P, 2011, Corp Gov	57
Haniffa, RM, Cooke, TE, Culture, corporate governance and disclosure in Malaysian corporations (2002) Abacus, 38 (3), pp. 317–349	42	Khan HUZ, 2010, Int J Law Manage	56

Using VosViewer it was possible to analyze the keywords of the studies of the sample analyzed by carrying out two types of analysis: network analysis and overlay visualization. The first analysis allows to group the articles to identify the common topics investigated. The second analysis distinguishes the topics dealt with temporally, highlighting the topics recently investigated by scholars. Figure 2.6 reveals the results of the network analysis.

The network analysis identifies three specific clusters:

- In green the studies that are in continuity with the more traditional studies of corporate governance.

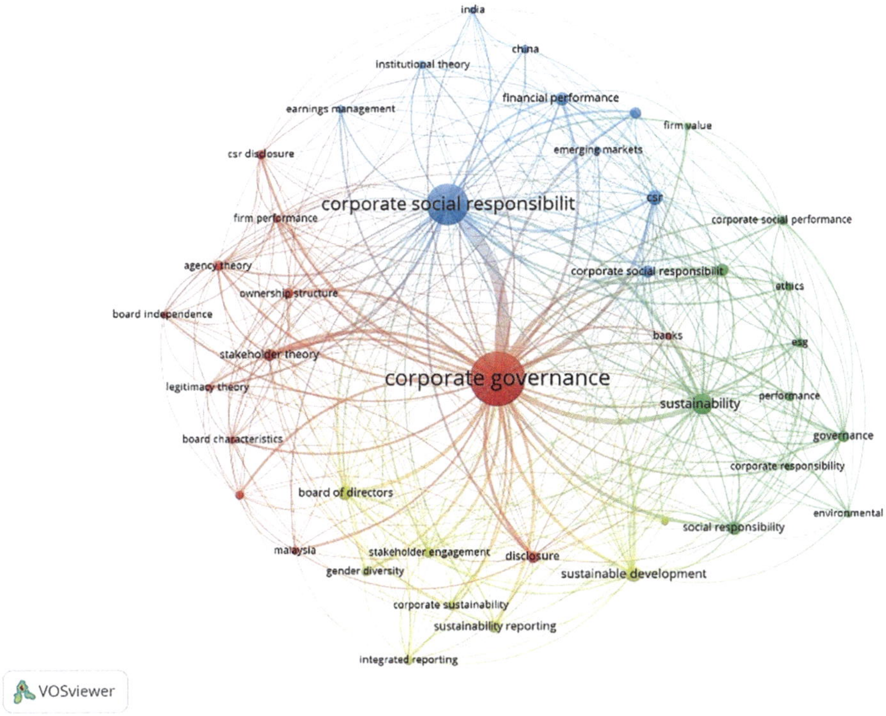

Fig. 2.5 Keyword analysis. Source: Author elaboration

- In blue are the studies that have investigated corporate governance from an accountability point of view.
- In red the contribution of governance to sustainability reporting models.

It is interesting to note how in the last 5 years the efforts of scholars have converged on accounting and disclosure.

Otherwise Fig. 2.7 shows the results of the overlay visualization.

As reported in the legend of the figure, the darker colors are associated with the keywords used at the beginning of the period examined, while the lighter colors tending towards yellow concern those found in more recent studies. In the first half of the period, the first studies investigating gender issues in the board of directors and how these influenced the company's orientation towards sustainable practices (Ben-Amar et al., 2017; Cucari et al., 2018; Gallego-Álvarez & Pucheta-Martínez, 2020; Haque & Jones, 2020). Furthermore, several scholars have analyzed the relationship between governance and the alignment of corporate reporting to the IIRC framework (Chaidali & Jones, 2017; Wang et al., 2020). Conversely, scholars have recently begun to investigate the effects produced by the pandemic period on the corporate governance and sustainability relationship (Chauhan et al., 2021; Sivaprasad & Mathew, 2021). It is interesting to see how some scholars have

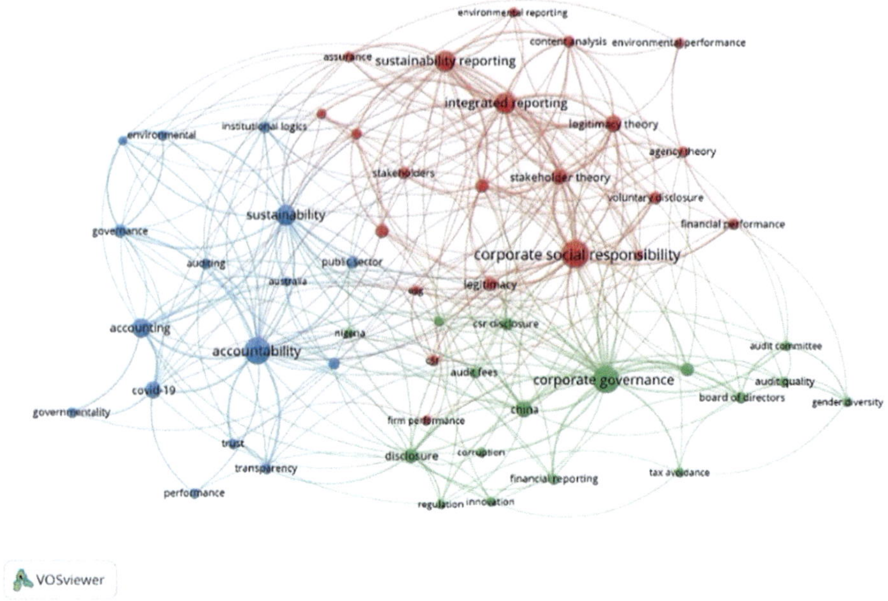

Fig. 2.6 Network analysis. Source: Author elaboration

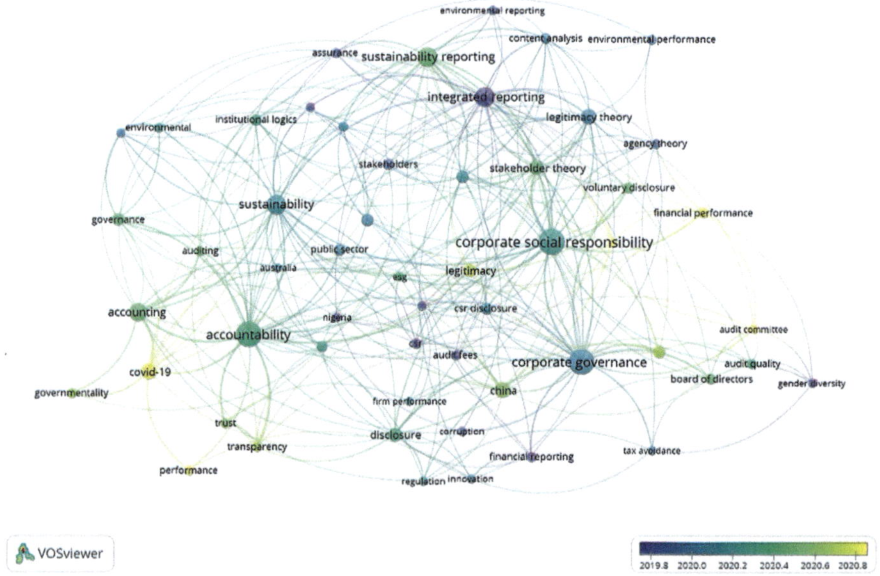

Fig. 2.7 Overlay visualization. Source: Author elaboration

begun to explore the topic from a different lens. Indeed, some studies have used the lens of institutional theory differently from other scholars who have used the theories discussed in the first chapter (Elijido-Ten et al., 2019; Ning et al., 2017; Wu et al., 2022). Finally, some studies have begun to investigate the influence of the control body (Jin et al., 2021; Nahar et al., 2020).

2.5.1 Accountability

The word responsibility can be declined in different ways and have different nuances. Depending on the nuances and meanings, if we refer to positive qualities, a moral obligation, or an imputation, different terms can be used: responsibility, liability, or accountability. It can refer in a general sense to responsibility about actions or facts committed. For example, the word liability disclaims liability in the legal sense.

The word accountability is also often used in different contexts, however, it is not possible to state that there is a single definition in the literature or corporate governance codes. Some scholars have it defined as:

> the mean by which individuals and organizations report to a recognized authority (or authorities) and are held responsible for their actions (Edwards & Hulme, 1996)

or

> to be accountable for one's activities is to explain the reasons for them and to supply the normative grounds whereby they may be justified (Edwards & Hulme, 1996)

Despite this, the word accountability is often associated with and contained in various definitions of corporate governance. For example, the definition of corporate governance given by the UK's Department for Business Innovation and Skills:

> the system by which companies are directed and controlled. It deals largely with the relationship between the constituent parts of a company—the directors, the board (and its sub-committees), and the shareholders. Transparency and accountability are the most important elements of good corporate governance.

The synthesis of the different configurations of accountability takes the form of a responsibility that the board has towards the different categories of stakeholders. The responsibility of the board manifests itself in greater transparency of its work both internally, to the shareholders, and towards the various stakeholders (Brennan & Solomon, 2008; Zahir-Ul-Hassan et al., 2016). A responsible board should therefore accurately inform about the decisions and actions implemented and should justify any risks taken or omissions.

Carroll and other authors suggest three visions of corporate accountability: communicative, phenomenological, and consequentialist view (Carroll & Olegario, 2020). The first perspective refers to studies that argue that the more a company discloses, the more responsible an organization is. According to these studies, companies that align themselves with reporting standards give an external signal that they want to meet the expectations of those concerned (Maroun, 2019; Chahed, 2021). However, some studies have criticized this assumption. In particular, evidence shows that disclosing information and having corporate accounts does not necessarily imply the demand for accountability of stakeholders (Kolk, 2008; Du Rietz, 2018). Criticism more emphasized by Dillard and Vinnari (Dillard & Vinnari, 2019) who speak about *Accounting-based accountability,* understood as a presumption of responsibility.

The second perspective associates accountability with the requests of stakeholders. Responsibility is therefore measured as gaps between what is material for the organization and what is material for the various stakeholders (Carroll & Olegario, 2020; Masiero et al., 2020). In this sense, the concept of accountability is linked with corporate reputation. Accountability could concern the improvement of the corporate reputation towards the various stakeholders (Le Breton-Miller & Miller, 2019). This, however, has led some to argue that reporting practices have the unique purpose of managing stakeholders rather than being accountable for their actions (Swift, 2001). The third perspective associates the concept of accountability with an ex-post evaluation. In this perspective, an organization can be defined as responsible only based on its actions (Carroll & Olegario, 2020).

The concept of accountability and the relationship between accountability and board has been the subject of discussion by various scholars over the past 40 years. The first studies indicated accountability as a tool for shareholders to reduce the risk of individual behavior by agents (Miller, 2002; Roberts et al., 2005; Brennan & Solomon, 2008).

After the crisis of the first decade of 2000, discussions began on whether corporate government were largely accountable. Based on a broader concept of governance, accountability has been placed within the characteristics that can categorize corporate governance as "good."

"Good" governance can be identified as a combination of mechanisms and structures which, on the one hand, promote accountability and control processes and, on the other hand, are functional to the achievement of strategic objectives.

The studies included in the cluster have tried to detect the governance models as well as the characteristics that the board should assume to affect the level of accountability and transparency. Recent studies that have analyzed companies in the pandemic context have begun to investigate possible permanent changes to accountability processes. In particular, accounting, finance, and management scholars have investigated the governance levers on which to act to stimulate virtuous processes of accountability (Ayoko et al., 2021; Sivaprasad & Mathew, 2021; Pozzoli et al., 2022).

2.5.2 *Governance and Non-financial Reporting and Performance*

Since the board must also be accountable to the various stakeholders, a part of the literature investigating the information transparency of corporate governance has consolidated in recent years. Transparency which is aimed at mandatory information (financial reporting) and voluntary information (non-financial reporting). In recent years, virtuous boards have decided to disclose more information embracing ESG-related issues. This prompted scholars to delve into the topic by investigating the reasons that led the board to report non-mandatory information externally. For these researches, scholars have used various theories, some of which have already been discussed in the first chapter:

- Agency theory (Choi & Suh, 2019; Gallego-Álvarez & Pucheta-Martínez, 2020; Whitehead & Belghitar, 2022)
- Stakeholder theory (Alipour et al., 2019; Minutolo et al., 2019; Nadeem, 2020)
- Legitimacy theory (Velte et al., 2020; Velte & Stawinoga, 2020)
- Institutional theory (Gallego-Alvarez et al., 2017; Elijido-Ten et al., 2019)

Although various interpretations of the phenomenon have been used, the prevailing literature associates the board with an important role for corporate sustainability practices and reporting. Good governance is also the one that discloses more sustainability information and is more transparent. Several pieces of research evidence conducted in different contexts have demonstrated how necessary for transparent ESG disclosure is governance that is sensitive to ESG dynamics and forward-looking. Empirical evidence based on different reporting standards (IIRC, 2013; Global Reporting Initiative, 2016; Sustainability Accounting Standard Board, 2017) has shown that companies that are more aligned with the different standards and with a high quality of reporting are equipped with governance mechanisms aimed at satisfying the needs of the stakeholders.

Not only that, good governance also influences the company's sustainability performance. Recent studies have highlighted how much governance positively influences environmental performance, so much so as to open a line of research related to climate change performance (Ben-Amar et al., 2017; Elsayih et al., 2018; Elijido-Ten et al., 2019; Khan et al., 2019a, b; Kılıç & Kuzey, 2019). These studies agree that strategic management is crucial for the reduction of GHG emissions.

2.5.3 *Governance Structure*

The last cluster concerns the governance structure and mechanisms. The different models and the different characteristics of corporate governance can influence corporate choices and performance (Donnelly & Mulcahy, 2008; Lo & Wong, 2011; Zattoni & Van Ees, 2012). The analysis shows that in the field of sustainability, the scholars have mainly investigated the board of directors while recently it is developing a research vein on the audit committee and control systems.

Concerning the board of directors, the literature has found that the different composition of the board can affect the efficiency of the governance mechanism (Michelon & Parbonetti, 2012). The diversity of board members in terms of experience, gender, age, profession, culture, and nationality can represent a value and is to be preferred over boards characterized by a greater degree of homogeneity (Ntim et al., 2013). Recently, several pieces of evidence have demonstrated an influence on sustainability results mainly of boards of directors diversified by gender (Bravo & Alcaide-Ruiz, 2019; Khan et al., 2019a, b; Tingbani et al., 2020). These studies agree in enhancing some peculiar characteristics of the female gender would lead to greater sensitivity towards the issues of socio-environmental sustainability and orientation towards stakeholders (Haque, 2017; Lodhia et al., 2020).

Another feature investigated by scholars is the presence of independent directors. On this issue, unlike the gender parameter, scholars do not fully agree in attributing a decisive and significant impact to these categories of directors (Giannarakis et al., 2017; Katmon & Al-Farooque, 2019; Shan, 2019). Indeed, there is empirical evidence that has not provided evidence of a relationship between ESG results and independents. Additionally, other studies have tested for any differences in CSR performance or disclosure of firms where the posts of CEO and president are separate from those where they are not (Biswas et al., 2019; Husted & de Sousa-Filho, 2019; Lagasio & Cucari, 2019).

On the other hand, other studies, assuming the relevance of directors in handling financial and non-financial information, whether audit committees should also oversee corporate social responsibility disclosures have been a topic of recent professional and academic controversy (KPMG, 2017; Bravo & Reguera-Alvarado, 2019; El Gammal et al., 2020). Audit committees do, in fact, increasingly scrutinize the reporting process and are worried about the veracity of sustainability reporting (Dwekat et al., 2020). Evidence shows that the audit committee increases the credibility of sustainability reports (Al-Shaer & Zaman, 2018). These studies suggest that rather than focusing on governance mechanisms, companies could also act on control systems to improve the performance and credibility of ESG information.

2.5.4 Focus CSR Committee

ESG matters differ in nature from the financial issues traditionally dealt with by companies. To this end, specific skills are needed to understand and manage these issues. Above all, companies not used to handling ESG information have had to make organizational changes, some of these compulsorily due to the Non-Financial Reporting Directive (NFRD), in order to be able to externally disclose the information requested in general by stakeholders (and in some specific cases by the NFRD).

The governing bodies to govern these changes within corporate processes and management have delegated ESG matters. In particular, the internal constitution of corporate figures or bodies entrusted with ESG responsibilities is increasingly frequent. The establishment of CSR committees represents one of the changes in governance mechanisms caused by the attempt to integrate sustainability within the different levels of the value chain. Like other committees such as the audit committee or the remuneration committee, the CSR committee is generally composed of a group of directors who interface directly with the board (Shaukat et al., 2016).

These bodies have the task of guaranteeing adequate attention to ESG practices and communication aimed at improving corporate results. Furthermore, this committee has the task of interacting with and advising the board of directors on how corporate policies can be compliant and oriented towards sustainable development objectives.

However, some academics disagree with the prevailing position. They argue that the establishment of internal council committees would represent only a symbolic action rather than a substantive policy (Elmaghrabi, 2021). According to this minority opinion, to be sustainable, companies should invest more resources in different areas to improve socio-environmental performance (Hart, 1995).

The influence of the CSR committee on performance and disclosure is now being studied by international scholars. In the literature, there are works on the impact of the committee on disclosure, few on performance (Peters & Romi, 2014; Liao et al., 2015; Fuente et al., 2017; Martínez-Ferrero et al., 2020; Sadiq et al., 2020; Tingbani et al., 2020). In terms of disclosure, the CSR committee would guarantee stakeholders greater transparency of information and alignment with international standards (Manurung et al., 2018; Pizzi et al., 2022).

CSR committee can be a choice to manage a new and complex matter such as climate change risk mitigation (Kılıç & Kuzey, 2019; Cordova et al., 2020; Cosma et al., 2022). Regarding performance, there is evidence of a positive association in Europe between the existence of CSR committees and ESG performance (Baraibar-Diez & Odriozola, 2019) and in the North American context between the committee and social performance (Mallin & Michelon, 2011).

However, this mechanism of sustainable governance must be further studied by international scholars to better understand its potential and effectiveness. In fact, it is not clear how much the composition of the members of the committee can affect the effectiveness of the body. Due to the specific nature of the matter, it would be necessary for all or part of the directors to possess skills in various areas of sustainability in order to fully understand the phenomenon to select the best solutions from among the various alternatives. Furthermore, the effectiveness of a body, in addition to differing from company to company, could vary due to the different configurations of the Companies Governance Code of the different States.

References

Adams, C. A. (2017). Conceptualising the contemporary corporate value creation process. *Accounting, Auditing and Accountability Journal, 30*(4), 906–931.

Alipour, M., Ghanbari, M., Jamshidinavid, B., & Taherabadi, A. (2019). Does board independence moderate the relationship between environmental disclosure quality and performance? Evidence from static and dynamic panel data. *Corporate Governance (Bingley), 19*(3), 580–610.

Al-Shaer, H., & Zaman, M. (2018). Credibility of sustainability reports: The contribution of audit committees. *Business Strategy and the Environment, 27*(7), 973–986.

Aria, M., & Cuccurullo, C. (2017). bibliometrix: An R-tool for comprehensive science mapping analysis. *Journal of Informetrics, 11*(4), 959–975.

Ayoko, O. B., Caputo, A., & Mendy, J. (2021). Management research contributions to the COVID-19: A bibliometric literature review and analysis of the contributions from the Journal of Management & Organization. *Journal of Management & Organization, 27*(6), 1183–1209.

Baraibar-Diez, E., & Odriozola, M. D. (2019). CSR committees and their effect on ESG performance in UK, France, Germany, and Spain. *Sustainability (Switzerland), 11*(18).

Barnea, A., & Rubin, A. (2010). Corporate social responsibility as a conflict between shareholders. *Journal of Business Ethics, 97*(1), 71–86.

Bartolacci, F., Caputo, A., & Soverchia, M. (2020). Sustainability and financial performance of small and medium sized enterprises: A bibliometric and systematic literature review. *Business Strategy and the Environment, 29*(3), 1297–1309.

Bebbington, J., Österblom, H., Crona, B., Jouffray, J. B., Larrinaga, C., Russell, S., & Scholtens, B. (2019). Accounting and accountability in the anthropocene. *Accounting, Auditing and Accountability Journal, 33*(1), 152–177. https://doi.org/10.1108/AAAJ-11-2018-3745

Belloque, G., Linnenluecke, M. K., Marrone, M., Singh, A. K., & Xue, R. (2021). 55 years of abacus: Evolution of research streams and future research directions. *Abacus, 57*(3), 593–618.

Ben-Amar, W., Chang, M., & McIlkenny, P. (2017). Board gender diversity and corporate response to sustainability initiatives: Evidence from the carbon disclosure project. *Journal of Business Ethics, 142*(2), 369–383. https://doi.org/10.1007/s10551-015-2759-1

Bertini, U. (1995). Scritti di politica aziendale. In *Studi di economia e politica aziendale*. Giappichelli.

Biswas, P. K., Roberts, H., & Whiting, R. H. (2019). The impact of family vs non-family governance contingencies on CSR reporting in Bangladesh. *Management Decision, 57*(10), 2758–2781.

Bravo, F., & Alcaide-Ruiz, M. D. (2019). The disclosure of financial forward-looking information: Does the financial expertise of female directors make a difference? *Gender in Management, 34*(2), 140–156.

Bravo, F., & Reguera-Alvarado, N. (2019). Sustainable development disclosure: Environmental, social, and governance reporting and gender diversity in the audit committee. *Business Strategy and the Environment, 28*(2), 418–429.

Brennan, N. M., & Solomon, J. (2008). Corporate governance, accountability and mechanisms of accountability: An overview. *Accounting, Auditing & Accountability Journal, 21*(7), 885–906.

Capurro, R., Fiorentino, R., Garzella, S., & Morrone, C. (2020). The creation of value: The necessary completion of the corporate control and communication system. *Management Control, 2*, 37–55. https://doi.org/10.3280/MACO2020-002003

Caputo, A., Marzi, G., Pellegrini, M. M., & Rialti, R. (2018). *Conflict management in family: A bibliometric analysis and systematic*. https://doi.org/10.1108/IJCMA-02-2018-0027.

Caputo, A., Pizzi, S., Pellegrini, M. M., & Dabić, M. (2021). Digitalization and business models: Where are we going? A science map of the field. *Journal of Business Research, 123*, 489–501.

Carroll, A. B. (1991). The pyramid of corporate social responsibility: Toward the moral management of organizational stakeholders. *Business Horizons, 34*(4), 39–48.

Carroll, C. E., & Olegario, R. (2020). Pathways to corporate accountability: Corporate reputation and its alternatives. *Journal of Business Ethics, 163*(2), 173–181.

Castellani, G. (2015). *Responsabilità sociale d'impresa. Ragioni, azioni e reporting*. Maggioli Editore.

Chahed, Y. (2021). Words and numbers: Financialization and accounting standard setting in the United Kingdom. *Contemporary Accounting Research, 38*(1), 302–337.

Chaidali, P., & Jones, M. J. (2017). It's a matter of trust: Exploring the perceptions of integrated reporting preparers. *Critical Perspectives on Accounting, 48*, 1–20.

Chauhan, A., Jakhar, S. K., & Chauhan, C. (2021). The interplay of circular economy with industry 4.0 enabled smart city drivers of healthcare waste disposal. *Journal of Cleaner Production, 279*. https://doi.org/10.1016/j.jclepro.2020.123854

Choi, H., & Suh, S. (2019). The effect of financial reporting quality on CEO compensation structure: Evidence from accounting comparability. *Journal of Accounting and Public Policy, 38*(5).

Cordova, C., Zorio-Grima, A., & Merello, P. (2020). Contextual and corporate governance effects on carbon accounting and carbon performance in emerging economies. *Corporate Governance (Bingley), 21*(3), 536–550.

Coronella, S., Caputo, F., Leopizzi, R., & Venturelli, A. (2018). Corporate social responsibility in Economia Aziendale scholars' theories: A taxonomic perspective. *Meditari Accountancy Research, 26*(4), 640–656. https://doi.org/10.1108/MEDAR-03-2017-0124

Cosma, S., Principale, S., & Venturelli, A. (2022). Sustainable governance and climate-change disclosure in European banking: The role of the corporate social responsibility committee. *Corporate Governance (Bingley), 22*(6), 1345–1369.

Cucari, N., Esposito De Falco, S., & Orlando, B. (2018). Diversity of board of directors and environmental social governance: Evidence from Italian listed companies. *Corporate Social Responsibility and Environmental Management, 25*(3), 250–266.

De Villiers, C., & Hsiao, P.-C. K. (2018). Why organizations voluntarily report – Agency theory. In *Sustainability accounting and integrated reporting* (pp. 49–56). Routledge.

De Villiers, C., & Marques, A. (2016). Corporate social responsibility, country-level predispositions, and the consequences of choosing a level of disclosure. *Accounting and Business Research, 46*(2), 167–195.

Deegan, C. M. (2019). Legitimacy theory: Despite its enduring popularity and contribution, time is right for a necessary makeover. *Accounting Auditing & Accountability Journal, 32*(8), 2307–2329.

Deegan, C., Rankin, M., & Tobin, J. (2002). An examination of the corporate social and environmental disclosures of BHP from 1983–1997: A test of legitimacy theory. *Accounting, Auditing & Accountability Journal, 15*(3), 312–343. MCB UP Ltd.

Di Cagno, N., Adamo, S., & Giaccari, F. (2019). *L'Azienda. Finalità - Struttura - Amministrazione*. Cacucci.

Dillard, J., & Vinnari, E. (2019). Critical dialogical accountability: From accounting-based accountability to accountability-based accounting. *Critical Perspectives on Accounting, 62*, 16–38.

Donaldson, T., & Preston, L. E. (1995). The stakeholder theory of the corporation: Concepts, evidence, and implications. *The Academy of Management Review, 20*(1), 65. https://doi.org/10.2307/258887

Donnelly, R., & Mulcahy, M. (2008). Board structure, ownership, and voluntary disclosure in Ireland. *Corporate Governance: An International Review, 16*(5), 416–429. Blackwell Publishing.

Du Rietz, S. (2018). Information vs knowledge: Corporate accountability in environmental, social, and governance issues. *Accounting Auditing & Accountability Journal, 31*(2), 586–607.

Dwekat, A., Seguí-Mas, E., Tormo-Carbó, G., & Carmona, P. (2020). Corporate governance configurations and corporate social responsibility disclosure: Qualitative comparative analysis of audit committee and board characteristics. *Corporate Social Responsibility and Environmental Management, 27*(6), 2879–2892. https://doi.org/10.1002/CSR.2009

Edwards, M., & Hulme, D. (1996). Too close for comfort? The impact of official aid on nongovernmental organizations. *World Development, 24*(6), 961–973.

El Gammal, W., Yassine, N., Fakih, K., & El-Kassar, A. N. (2020). The relationship between CSR and corporate governance moderated by performance and board of directors' characteristics. *Journal of Management and Governance, 24*(2), 411–430.

Elijido-Ten, E. O., Datt, R. R., Luo, L., Tang, Q., Zamora-Ramírez, C., González-González, J. M., & Jubb, C. (2019). Do you manage what you measure? Investor views on the question of climate actions with empirical results from the Swiss pension fund and insurance sector. *Journal of Business Ethics, 32*(2), 369–383.

Elmaghrabi, M. E. (2021). CSR committee attributes and CSR performance: UK evidence. *Corporate Governance (Bingley), 21*(5), 892–919.

Elsayih, J., Tang, Q., & Lan, Y.-C. (2018). Corporate governance and carbon transparency: Australian experience. *Accounting Research Journal, 31*(3), 405–422.

Falagas, M. E., Pitsouni, E. I., Malietzis, G. A., & Pappas, G. (2008). Comparison of PubMed, Scopus, Web of Science, and Google Scholar: Strengths and weaknesses. *FASEB Journal: Official Publication of the Federation of American Societies for Experimental Biology, 22*(2), 338–342.

Freeman, R. E. (1984). *Strategic management: A stakeholder approach*. Pitman.

Freeman, R. E., Harrison, J. S., Wicks, A. C., Parmar, B. L., & De Colle, S. (2010). *Stakeholder theory: The state of the art*.

Fuente, J. A., García-Sánchez, I. M., & Lozano, M. B. (2017). The role of the board of directors in the adoption of GRI guidelines for the disclosure of CSR information. *Journal of Cleaner Production, 141*, 737–750.

Galeotti, M. (2006). *Governo dell'azienda e indicatori di performance*. Giappichelli Editore.

Gallego-Álvarez, I., & Pucheta-Martínez, M. C. (2020). Corporate social responsibility reporting and corporate governance mechanisms: An international outlook from emerging countries. *Business Strategy and Development, 3*(1), 77–97.

Gallego-Alvarez, I., Ortas, E., Vicente-Villardón, J. L., & Álvarez Etxeberria, I. (2017). Institutional constraints, stakeholder pressure and corporate environmental reporting policies. *Business Strategy and the Environment, 26*(6), 807–825.

Garcia Sanchez, I.-M., Rodriguez Dominguez, L., & Gallego Alvarez, I. (2011). Corporate governance and strategic information on the internet: A study of Spanish listed companies. *Accounting Auditing & Accountability Journal, 24*(4), 471–501.

Garzella, S. (2018). L'azienda e la corporate social responsibility: Approfondimenti dottrinali e riflessioni gestionali. *L'azienda e la corporate social responsibility*, 1–124.

Giannarakis, G., Konteos, G., Sariannidis, N., & Chaitidis, G. (2017). The relation between voluntary carbon disclosure and environmental performance: The case of S&P 500. *International Journal of Law and Management, 59*(6), 784–803.

Global Reporting Initiative. (2016). *Introduction to the GRI standards*.

Guthrie, J., & Parker, L. D. (1989). Corporate social reporting: A rebuttal of legitimacy theory. *Accounting and Business Research, 19*(76), 343–352.

Halal, W. E. (1978). Beyond the profit motive: The post-industrial corporation. *Technological Forecasting and Social Change, 12*(1), 13–29.

Haque, F. (2017). The effects of board characteristics and sustainable compensation policy on carbon performance of UK firms. *British Accounting Review, 49*(3), 347–364.

Haque, F., & Jones, M. J. (2020). European firms' corporate biodiversity disclosures and board gender diversity from 2002 to 2016. *British Accounting Review, 52*(2).

Harjoto, M. A., & Jo, H. (2011). Corporate governance and CSR nexus. *Journal of Business Ethics, 100*(1), 45–67.

Hart, S. L. (1995). A natural-resource-based view of the firm. *The Academy of Management Review, 20*(4), 986.

Husted, B. W., & de Sousa-Filho, J. M. (2019). Board structure and environmental, social, and governance disclosure in Latin America. *Journal of Business Research, 102*, 220–227.

IIRC. (2013). *The international integrated reporting framework*. www.theiirc.org

Jain, T., & Jamali, D. (2016). Looking inside the black box: The effect of corporate governance on corporate social responsibility. *Corporate Governance: An International Review, 24*(3), 253–273.

Jin, Q., Jin, Y., Tian, G. G., & Xuan, Y. (2021). Does internal corporate governance complement or substitute for external auditing? Evidence from China's anti-corruption campaign. *Abacus – A Journal of Accounting Finance And Business Studies, 57*(1), 153–182.

Katmon, N., & Al-Farooque, O. (2019). The reciprocal relationship between earnings management, disclosure quality and board independence: UK evidence. *Research in World Economy, 10*(5), 63–80.

Khan, A., Muttakin, M. B., & Siddiqui, J. (2013). Corporate governance and corporate social responsibility disclosures: Evidence from an emerging economy. *Journal of Business Ethics, 114*(2), 207–223. https://doi.org/10.1007/s10551-012-1336-0

Khan, H. Z., Bose, S., & Johns, R. (2019a). Regulatory influences on CSR practices within banks in an emerging economy: Do banks merely comply? *Critical Perspectives on Accounting*. https://doi.org/10.1016/j.cpa.2019.102096

Khan, I., Khan, I., & Senturk, I. (2019b). Board diversity and quality of CSR disclosure: Evidence from Pakistan. *Corporate Governance (Bingley), 19*(6), 1187–1203.

Kılıç, M., & Kuzey, C. (2019). The effect of corporate governance on carbon emission disclosures: Evidence from Turkey. *International Journal of Climate Change Strategies and Management, 11*(1), 35–53.

Kolk, A. (2008). Sustainability, accountability and corporate governance: Exploring multinationals' reporting practices. *Business Strategy and the Environment, 17*(1), 1–15. https://doi.org/10.1002/BSE.511

KPMG. (2017). *Audit committee handbook*. KPMG Audit Committee Institute. https://assets.kpmg/content/dam/kpmg/pdf/2014/12/audit-committee-handbook.pdf

Lagasio, V., & Cucari, N. (2019). Corporate governance and environmental social governance disclosure: A meta-analytical review. *Corporate Social Responsibility and Environmental Management, 26*(4), 701–711.

Le Breton-Miller, I., & Miller, D. (2019). Ideals-based accountability and reputation in select family firms. *Journal of Business Ethics*.

Liao, L., Luo, L., & Tang, Q. (2015). Gender diversity, board independence, environmental committee and greenhouse gas disclosure. *British Accounting Review, 47*(4), 409–424.

Lo, A. W. Y., & Wong, R. M. K. (2011). An empirical study of voluntary transfer pricing disclosures in China. *Journal of Accounting and Public Policy, 30*(6), 607–628.

Lodhia, S., Kaur, A., & Stone, G. (2020). The use of social media as a legitimation tool for sustainability reporting: A study of the top 50 Australian stock exchange (ASX) listed companies. *Meditari Accountancy Research, 28*(4), 613–632.

Lombardi, R. (2021). *The going-concern-principle in non-financial disclosure* (pp. 1–100). https://doi.org/10.1007/978-3-030-81127-3

Mallin, C. A., & Michelon, G. (2011). Board reputation attributes and corporate social performance: An empirical investigation of the US best corporate citizens. *Accounting and Business Research, 41*(2), 119–144.

Mancini, D., Lamboglia, R., Garzella, S., & Fiorentino, R. (2016). Strategie di sostenibilità: dalle motivazioni ai sistemi di misurazione della performance. *Strategie di sostenibilità: dalle motivazioni ai sistemi di misurazione della performance*, 116–142.

Manurung, D. T. H., Hardika, A. L., Hapsari, D. W., & Sebayang, M. M. (2018). The role of corporate governance and environmental committees on greenhouse gas disclosure. *Journal of Environmental Management and Tourism, 9*(7), 1403–1413.

Marchi, L. (2019). Governo delle aziende e creazione di valore: da una prospettiva finanziaria ad una prospettiva economico-sociale. *Management Control, 1*.

Maroun, W. (2019). Does external assurance contribute to higher quality integrated reports? *Journal of Accounting and Public Policy, 38*(4).

Martínez-Ferrero, J., Lozano, M. B., & Vivas, M. (2020). The impact of board cultural diversity on a firm's commitment toward the sustainability issues of emerging countries: The mediating effect of a CSR committee. *Corporate Social Responsibility and Environmental Management*, 675–685.

Masiero, E., Arkhipova, D., Massaro, M., & Bagnoli, C. (2020). Corporate accountability and stakeholder connectivity. A case study. *Meditari Accountancy Research, 28*(5), 803–831.

McWilliams, A., & Siegel, D. (2001). Corporate social responsibility: A theory of the firm perspective. *The Academy of Management Review, 26*(1), 117. https://doi.org/10.2307/259398

Michelon, G., & Parbonetti, A. (2012). The effect of corporate governance on sustainability disclosure. *Journal of Management and Governance, 16*(3), 477–509. https://doi.org/10.1007/s10997-010-9160-3

Miller, J. L. (2002). The board as a monitor of organizational activity: The applicability of agency theory to nonprofit boards. *Nonprofit Management and Leadership, 12*(4), 429–450. https://doi.org/10.1002/NML.12407

Minutolo, M. C., Kristjanpoller, W. D., & Stakeley, J. (2019). Exploring environmental, social, and governance disclosure effects on the S&P 500 financial performance. *Business Strategy and the Environment, 28*(6), 1083–1095.

Mongeon, P., & Paul-Hus, A. (2015). The journal coverage of Web of Science and Scopus: A comparative analysis. *Scientometrics, 106*(1), 213–228.

Nadeem, M. (2020). Corporate governance and supplemental environmental projects: A restorative justice approach. *Journal of Business Ethics.*

Nahar, S., Azim, M. I., & Hossain, M. M. (2020). Risk disclosure and risk governance characteristics: Evidence from a developing economy. *International Journal of Accounting and Information Management, 28*(4), 577–605.

Ning, Y., Xiao, Z., & Lee, J. (2017). Shareholders and managers: Who care more about corporate diversity and employee benefits? *Journal of Management and Governance, 21*(1), 93–118.

Ntim, C. G., Lindop, S., & Thomas, D. A. (2013). Corporate governance and risk reporting in South Africa: A study of corporate risk disclosures in the pre- and post-2007/2008 global financial crisis periods. *International Review of Financial Analysis, 30*, 363–383.

Onida, P. (1971). *Economia d'azienda.* UTET. https://books.google.it/books?id=lJlOPQAACAAJ

Peters, G. F., & Romi, A. M. (2014). Does the voluntary adoption of corporate governance mechanisms improve environmental risk disclosures? Evidence from greenhouse gas emission accounting. *Journal of Business Ethics, 125*(4), 637–666.

Pizzi, S., Principale, S., & de Nuccio, E. (2022). Material sustainability information and reporting standards. Exploring the differences between GRI and SASB. *Meditari Accountancy Research.*

Pozzoli, M., Pagani, A., & Paolone, F. (2022). The impact of audit committee characteristics on ESG performance in the European Union member states: Empirical evidence before and during the COVID-19 pandemic. *Journal of Cleaner Production, 371*, 133411.

Rezaee, Z., & Tuo, L. (2017). Voluntary disclosure of non-financial information and its association with sustainability performance. *Advances in Accounting, 39*, 47–59.

Ricci, F., Scafarto, V., Ferri, S., & Tron, A. (2020). Value relevance of digitalization: The moderating role of corporate sustainability. An empirical study of Italian listed companies. *Journal of Cleaner Production, 276*, 123282.

Roberts, J., McNulty, T., & Stiles, P. (2005). Beyond agency conceptions of the work of the non-executive director: Creating accountability in the boardroom. *British Journal of Management, 16*(SPEC. ISS), S5–S26.

Rossi, M., Festa, G., Chouaibi, S., Fait, M., & Papa, A. (2021). The effects of business ethics and corporate social responsibility on intellectual capital voluntary disclosure. *Journal of Intellectual Capital, 22*(7), 1–23.

Sadiq, M., Singh, J., Raza, M., & Mohamad, S. (2020). The impact of environmental, social and governance index on firm value: Evidence from Malaysia. *International Journal of Energy Economics and Policy, 10*(5), 555–562.

Shan, Y. G. (2019). Do corporate governance and disclosure tone drive voluntary disclosure of related-party transactions in China? *Journal of International Accounting, Auditing and Taxation, 34*, 30–48.

Shaukat, A., Qiu, Y., & Trojanowski, G. (2016). Board attributes, corporate social responsibility strategy, and corporate environmental and social performance. *Journal of Business Ethics, 135*(3), 569–585.

Sivaprasad, S., & Mathew, S. (2021). Corporate governance practices and the pandemic crisis: UK evidence. *Corporate Governance (Bingley), 21*(6), 983–995.

Sustainability Accounting Standard Board. (2017). *SASB conceptual framework*. https://www.sasb.org/wp-content/uploads/2020/02/SASB_Conceptual-Framework_WATERMARK.pdf

Swift, T. (2001). Trust, reputation and corporate accountability to stakeholders. *Business Ethics: A European Review, 10*(1), 16–26.

Tingbani, I., Chithambo, L., Tauringana, V., & Papanikolaou, N. (2020). Board gender diversity, environmental committee and greenhouse gas voluntary disclosures. *Business Strategy and the Environment.* https://doi.org/10.1002/bse.2495

Velte, P., & Stawinoga, M. (2020). Do chief sustainability officers and CSR committees influence CSR-related outcomes? A structured literature review based on empirical-quantitative research findings. *Journal of Management Control, 31*(4), 333–377.

Velte, P., Stawinoga, M., & Lueg, R. (2020). Carbon performance and disclosure: A systematic review of governance-related determinants and financial consequences. *Journal of Cleaner Production, 254*, 120063. Elsevier.

Wang, R., Zhou, S., & Wang, T. (2020). Corporate governance, integrated reporting and the use of credibility-enhancing mechanisms on integrated reports. *European Accounting Review, 29*(4), 631–663.

Whitehead, M., & Belghitar, Y. (2022). Responding to a corruption crisis through disclosure and remedial action: The case of Petrobras. *The British Accounting Review, 54*(5), 101119.

Wu, W., Liang, Z., & Zhang, Q. (2022). Technological capabilities, technology management and economic performance: The complementary roles of corporate governance and institutional environment. *Journal of Knowledge Management, 26*(9), 2416–2439.

Ye, N., Kueh, T. B., Hou, L., Liu, Y., & Yu, H. (2020). A bibliometric analysis of corporate social responsibility in sustainable development. *Journal of Cleaner Production, 272*, 122679.

Zahir-Ul-Hassan, M. K., Minnaar, R. A., & Vosselman, E. (2016). Governance and control as mediating instruments in an inter-firm relationship: Towards collaboration or transactions? *Accounting and Business Research, 46*(4), 365–389.

Zattoni, A., & Van Ees, H. (2012). How to contribute to the development of a global understanding of corporate governance? Reflections from submitted and published articles in CGIR. *Corporate Governance: An International Review, 20*(1), 106–118.

Chapter 3
The Current Scenario on Sustainable Corporate Governance: Theoretical and Practical Evidence

Keywords Governance code · Sustainable corporate governance · Corporate sustainability due diligence · Sustainable corporate governance directive

3.1 Introduction

In the first chapter, some governance models widespread in the main countries of the European continent were exposed. Through culture and tradition, different models have developed in various European countries. The differences have also been enhanced by a very light European regulation leaving a lot of power to national regulations. The next figure highlights the different configurations envisaged by the various European states.

Throughout the chapter, the various national and European regulations about corporate governance are presented. Furthermore, Europe's attempts to coordinate and standardize the regulation of corporate governance are highlighted. Recently, Europe's attention has focused on the integration of sustainability also in corporate governance, following what has been suggested by scholars and international organizations.

In 2017, the publication of the recommendations of the Task Force on Climate-related Financial Disclosures (TCFD 2017) was significant. Although it is a document aimed at supporting companies in disclosing the risks of climate change as well as managing the risks and opportunities deriving from the average rise in global temperature, it has also had an impact on the issue of corporate governance. The Task Force on climate change has identified four areas necessary to manage climate change-related risks and opportunities and to disclose the necessary information to investors and they are: governance, strategy, risk management and metrics and target. Fundamental to an effective management of risks and opportunities is that the topics must primarily be discussed by the top management so that they can define strategies that also include the topics in question within them.

The European Commission has formally decided to follow the approach of the Climate Change Task Force to the point of making explicit references to it both in the

S. Principale, *Fostering Sustainability in Corporate Governance*, SIDREA Series in Accounting and Business Administration,
https://doi.org/10.1007/978-3-031-30354-8_3

drafting of the Corporate Sustainability Reporting Directive (CSRD) and in the first drafts defined by EFRAG.

3.2 Sustainability and Codes of Conduct

Broad freedom is given to Member States in terms of corporate governance regulation. The first European corporate governance code dates back to 1992 with the introduction of the Cadbury Code in the United Kingdom (Cadbury, 1992). The latter paved the way for the adoption of corporate governance codes in other European countries as well.

If, on the one hand, Europe supports the importance of a sustainable corporate governance that also has responsibility for sustainable issues, on the other we find that even at the level of national corporate governance codes there are already some virtuous examples of CSR integration. Although in different ways, several recent updates of the individual national codes have introduced obligations or recommendations for administrators (AFEP & Medef, 2020; Comision Nacional del Mercado de Valores, 2020; EU Commission, 2021; Financial Reporting Council, 2018).

The following table summarizes some areas present in the codes of the United Kingdom, Germany, France, Italy, and Spain (Table 3.1).

Following the example of the UK and Spain, the recent update of the Corporate Governance Code in Italy (2020) has introduced the concept of sustainable success. It takes the form of "the objective that guides the action of the administrative body and which takes the form of the creation of long-term value for the benefit of the shareholders, taking into account the interests of the company" (Comitato Corporate Governance, 2020). Attention to sustainable issues is also recommended in the German and French codes. In particular, the word sustainability/sustainable success is not present in the French Code, nevertheless explicit reference is made to the social and environmental spheres. Already in 2001, *Loi sur les nouvelles règulations it is economical* (NRE) required information on how environmental and social factors were considered in company management to be included in the management report (Assonime, 2021).

In all five countries considered, the Codes promote dialogue with stakeholders. In fact, one of the tasks of the board is to involve the various stakeholders. On this point, some argue that attention to stakeholders is based more on issues of risk management, to generate long-term value, rather than ethics.

Table 3.1 Sustainable issues in European codes of conduct

Field	UK	Germany	France	Italy	Spain
Sustainability	x	x	x	x	x
Stakeholders	x	x	x	x	x
Gender balance	x	x	x	x	x
CSR committee	0	0	0	0	x

About gender, there are specific references and recommendations in the Codes considered so that both genders are adequately represented on boards. The German and Italian Codes indicate a minimum quota of female quotas within the board, respectively, 30% of women on the Supervisory Board in the first case, one third on the board of directors in the second (Assonime, 2021).

Finally, of interest is the case of Spain which in the Code, in matters of sustainability, indicates that sustainability issues can be delegated and addressed by a committee. Specifically, the duties of the committee, whether pre-existing or not, would include the monitoring of corporate communication, the assessment that social and environmental policies are consistent with what has been defined strategically and that the company relates to stakeholders.

3.3 European Harmonization Policies and Corporate Governance Directive

Although, as explained, the matter of Corporate Governance has been regulated by the individual European States through the various codes of corporate governance, the European Union in its recent history has tried to give a common direction and to harmonize corporate law (Zattoni, 2020). The European Union has undertaken some actions in order to achieve a double objective. On the one hand, an attempt has been made to increase the comparability between companies which favors the assessments of investors or other interested parties. On the other hand, by standardizing the regulatory system of the different Member States, we want to avoid that regulation is a factor that could discourage companies from establishing themselves in States where regulation is more stringent (Bosetti, 2017). Leaving ample flexibility to the Member States, the European Union has carried out a series of interventions over the years which have been particularly concentrated in the 2000s.

Two-tier board structure of the board of directors to the detriment of the unitary one. The suggested configuration envisaged the presence of a supervisory board and an executive board with the first having the task of appointing executive directors and controlling them while the second body was assigned the role of the administration. The attempt to bring the rules of the member countries closer to those present in the German and Dutch context, however, did not have a positive outcome.

Recent regulatory interventions have affected some specific areas (Bosetti, 2017):

- The involvement of shareholders (Directive 2007/36/EC, Directive 201/828/EU)
- The bodies and processes of administration and control
- Information transparency (Transparency Directive 2004/109/EC, Directive 2006/46/EC, Directive 2013/50/EU, Recommendation 2014/208/EU)
- Legal auditing (Directive 84/253/EEC, Directive 2014/56/EU, Regulation No. 537/2014/EU)
- The stability of the financial markets and the quality of the services offered to savers or investors (Directive 2014/56/EU, Regulation 600/2014/EU)

As the list shows, the interventions were diverse and touched on different areas. Focusing on the area of transparency, it is in this area where the major regulatory acts have occurred over time. Corporate governance requires a high degree of transparency regarding the system adopted by the company as well as the roles, offices, and responsibilities assumed by the various components. It is also required that information relating to economic, social, and environmental activities and results be communicated. These communications are for the protection of investors and stakeholders so that information asymmetries are reduced and they are fully aware of the facts of company management.

(Transparency) and the subsequent update in Directive 2013/50/EU (Transparency II) are fully included. The regulations introduced obligations for listed companies in terms of communications and documents that they had to periodically publish to increase the efficiency of the markets and for a correct allocation of resources. The Transparency Directive envisaged the periodic obligation for listed companies to present certain economic-financial documents: annual financial reports, half-yearly financial report, and interim management reports. The latter were subsequently abolished by Transparency II which, unlike the previous one, intervened to simplify the fulfilments deemed too demanding and costly, above all for smaller companies.

Another significant stage concerned Directive 2006/46/EC with which listed companies are required to include in a section of the management report or in an attached document to be published together with the annual report or on the corporate website, a declaration on the corporate governance. Certain minimum information is required within the corporate governance statement:

- The corporate governance code that the company adopts
- Communications of governance choices that differ from the code to which reference is made
- Description of the internal control and risk management systems
- Any takeover bids
- Description of the functioning of the assembly and its powers, the rights of the shareholders
- Description of the main administrative and control bodies

The legislation provides for other obligations such as the communication of significant transactions with related parties.

Directive 2013/34/EU requires listed companies to adopt national codes of conduct or other voluntary basic regulations. Subsequently, through recommendation 2014/208/EU, the principle of "comply or explain" was established according to which the reasons that led the company to derogate from or deviate from the recommendation must be disclosed. The national codes, in fact, aim to identify the principles of good governance since it is considered that a governance that follows good practices can better manage the company, guaranteeing its competitiveness and long-term sustainability. Therefore, the rationale of the principle is to prevent companies from deviating from the good practices present in the codes of conduct unless there are precise reasons discussed within the board.

These are associated with the new provisions relating to the development of practices oriented towards the principles of sustainability and sustainable development.

3.4 European Union and Sustainability

The European Union has distinguished itself in recent years for its profound attention to the issues of social and environmental sustainability. The European Commission and the Member States have decided to establish themselves as leading countries towards the process of sustainable development in compliance with the agreements signed in the 2030 Agenda or in recent international events such as COP27. The commitment to sustainable development issues and to the 17 Sustainable Development Goals (SDGs) has materialized in the definition and publication of a series of policies and regulations coordinated with each other according to a precise design. The regulation has had an impact on European companies, especially large ones, since without the involvement of the private sector the achievement of ambitious objectives is unthinkable.

The project of the European Commission has had several stages in recent years. In 2018, the EU Action plan on sustainable finance was published which identified the measures to be taken to build a financial system capable of contributing to the objectives of the 2030 Agenda. In particular, the plan included ten actions which constituted the strengths of the European strategy:

1. Establishing an EU classification system for sustainable activities
2. Creating standards and labels for green financial products
3. Fostering investment in sustainable projects
4. Incorporating sustainability when providing financial advice
5. Developing sustainability benchmarks
6. Better integrating sustainability in ratings and market research
7. Clarifying institutional investors' and asset managers' duties
8. Incorporating sustainability in prudential requirements
9. Strengthening sustainability disclosure and accounting rule-making
10. Fostering sustainable corporate governance and attenuating short-termism in capital markets (EU Commission, 2018)

The author underline three actions. The first is Action 1, which is the definition of an EU Taxonomy. Taxonomy is a system that classifies economic activities according to their degree of environmental sustainability. In particular, it strictly defines the list of green activities that contribute to environmental sustainability by differentiating them from those that hinder it and some requirements in terms of environmental performance for companies or types of financial products. This was determined based on six environmental objectives:

- Climate change mitigation
- Adaptation to climate change
- Sustainable use and protection of water and marine resources
- The transition towards the circular economy, also regarding waste reduction and recycling
- Pollution prevention and control
- Protection of biodiversity and the health of ecosystems

The second action has the objective of encouraging reporting systems aimed at improving disclosure on non-financial matters and above all relating to climate change.

A first relevant reform was the introduction into the European regulatory context of Directive 95/2014/EU or Non-Financial Reporting Directive (NFRS). The Directive required companies that exceeded certain size limits to publish the Non-Financial Statement (in a separate document or together with the management statement) containing information about the environment, social, employees, anti-corruption, and compliance with human rights.

In its first formulation, the Directive had some limitations highlighted by accounting scholars. In fact, although the NFRD has stimulated the amount of information, on the other hand, problems related to the standardization and comparability of information have arisen (La Torre et al., 2020; Venturelli et al., 2020). Limits that the CSRD aims to overcome. The new features of the Directive include:

- Expansion of the obligations which will also extend to listed SMEs
- Development of European reporting standards developed by the European Financial Reporting Advisory Group (EFRAG)
- Explanation of the principle of double materiality
- Digitization of information according to a digital taxonomy
- Obligation to sworn reports

These are just some of the major demands introduced by the CSRD.

3.5 EU Sustainable Corporate Governance

In the ten actions defined by the EU Action Plan, corporate governance is one of the fundamental levers identified by the European Commission to promote sustainable growth of the economy. As highlighted in the previous paragraph, action 10 concerns interventions aimed at stimulating sustainable corporate governance. Businesses play an important role in achieving the sustainable development goals. Therefore, the European Commission maintains that corporate governance must favor the processes of sustainable growth of the economic system. The top corporate level has the power to plan and outline strategies to introduce sustainability into corporate business models, develop green technologies, or improve risk management practices.

Some are the reasons that led the European authority to decide to plan some interventions in support of sustainable corporate governance. A recent study by Ernest Young on European companies has highlighted some critical issues by suggesting some interventions by the European legislator. Based on the literature on the topic and on the data obtained from the administration of surveys, the report highlights some factors that limit the proactive action of corporate governance. Seven factors influence the work of governance (Ernst and Young, 2020):

- Companies are oriented towards maximizing short-term value for shareholders
- Investor pressures to achieve positive short-term results
- A lack of strategic perspective on ESG factors as well as a lack of interventions on the management of ESG risks
- Remuneration systems incentivize directors to create short-term shareholder value
- Lack of directors' sustainability skills
- Lack of effective stakeholder involvement
- Enforcement of directors' duty suggests acting in the short-term interest of the company rather than the long-term

The factors identified are an expression of the generalized short-sightedness of the corporate governance of European companies. The short-term orientation therefore clashes with sustainability which, on the contrary, by definition has characteristics that require a long-term oriented vision. This evidence would suggest that the Commission's intervention can stimulate companies to overcome the critical issues that impede good practices in sustainable development.

Furthermore, the report also highlights what has already been explained in the accounting studies which have had as their object the study of the implications of Directive 95/2014/EU (Doni et al., 2019; Muserra et al., 2020; Paolone et al., 2021; Veltri et al., 2020). The ESG reporting is closely linked to the issue of corporate governance. The limits that scholars and practitioners have found in corporate governance in a specular way have also been highlighted in the disclosure and reporting. Several studies support the lack of forward-looking information within corporate reporting systems (Beretta & Bozzolan, 2008; Cinquini et al., 2012; Mio et al., 2020; Stacchezzini et al., 2016). This information is necessary for investors to fully understand company dynamics and to be able to make performance comparisons. Therefore, the close connection between disclosure and governance underscores the limits of the latter in two ways. On the basis of this evidence, the Commission considered that corporate governance field is an area for possible regulatory interventions. In the 2018 communication, the commission predicted "*the possible need to require corporate boards to develop and disclose a sustainability strategy, including appropriate due diligence throughout the supply chain, and measurable sustainability targets; and (ii) the possible need to clarify the rules according to which directors are expected to act in the company's long-term interest*" (EU Commission, 2020a, b). The following paragraph analyzes in detail the proposal for a Directive which is part of the European Commission's plan for sustainable corporate governance.

3.6 Corporate Sustainability Due Diligence Proposal

3.6.1 Consultation

In a preliminary phase preceding the definition of the articles of the Directive, the European Commission has decided to open a consultation in the period from 26 February 2020 to 8 February 2021 to understand the opinions of the various stakeholders regarding potential interventions on corporate governance. The intention of the Commission was to receive the largest number of opinions from a broader category of subjects. The questionnaire included 26 questions, some of which have been inserted below:

- "Question 1: Do you think companies and their directors should take account of these interests (climate change, human rights, . . .) in corporate decisions alongside financial interests of shareholders, beyond what is currently required by EU law?
- Question 2: Do you think that an EU legal framework for supply chain due diligence to address adverse impacts on human rights and environmental issues should be developed?
- Question 6: Do you consider that corporate directors should be required by law to (1) identify the company's stakeholders and their interests, (2) to manage the risks for the company in relation to stakeholders and their interests, including on the long run (3) and to identify the opportunities arising from promoting stakeholders' interests?
- Question 7. Do you believe that corporate directors should be required by law to set up adequate procedures and where relevant, measurable (science–based) targets to ensure that possible risks and adverse impacts on stakeholders, i.e. are human rights, social, health and environmental impacts identified, prevented and addressed?
- Question 13. Do you consider that stakeholders, such as for example employees, the environment or people affected by the operations of the company as represented by civil society organizations should be given a role in the enforcement of directors' duty of care?
- Question 16: How could companies'—in particular smaller ones'—burden be reduced with respect to due diligence?
- Question 17: In your view, should the due diligence rules apply also to certain third-country companies which are not established in the EU but carry out (certain) activities in the EU?
- Question 20: Do you believe that the EU should require directors to establish and apply mechanisms or, where they already exist for employees for example, use existing information and consultation channels for engaging with stakeholders in this area?
- Question 22: Enhancing sustainability expertise in the board Current level of expertise of boards of directors does not fully support a shift towards sustainability, so action to enhance directors' competence in this area could be envisaged."

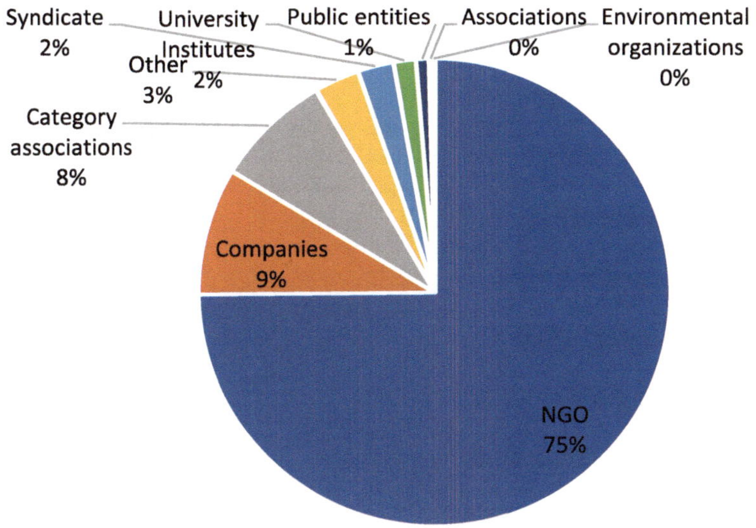

Fig. 3.1 Consultation participants. Source: Author elaboration

(available at. http://mneguidelines.oecd.org/OECD-submission-to-European-Commission-public-consultation-sustainable-corporate-governance.pdf).

The participation in the consultation was high, it was open and received a total of 473,461 valid comments. Different categories of stakeholders responded to the consultation. The contribution of a large number of comments also from citizens belonging to non-EU countries is interesting. If we exclude the high number of EU Citizens (296378) and non-EU Citizens (174919), the following figure summarizes the various categories attending (Fig. 3.1).

The high participation is a feeling of sensitivity about the theme that the European Commission intends to introduce. Furthermore, the presence of the issue of human rights could justify the high participation of non-governmental organizations (NGOs), which have always been at the forefront of the fight to ensure that human rights are respected in the world (Denedo et al., 2017, 2019).

France and Germany are the areas that have shown the greatest participation towards the consultation on the Sustainable Corporate Governance Directive. The opinion of Italian stakeholders was also well represented with about 31,832 comments preceded by the aforementioned France and Germany and the United Kingdom with 46,526 replies. Particular is the presence of replies received from non-EU subjects as reported in the case of Brazil (25,045 replies), Canada (19,403 replies), and the United States (16,322) (Fig. 3.2).

From the answers received, it is clear the need identified by the stakeholders to increase the regulation in terms of sustainable corporate governance and due diligence on human rights. More than 80% of respondents agree that it is important for administrators to deal with various ESG issues and that a framework for due diligence on human rights and environmental issues is defined. Just over 70%

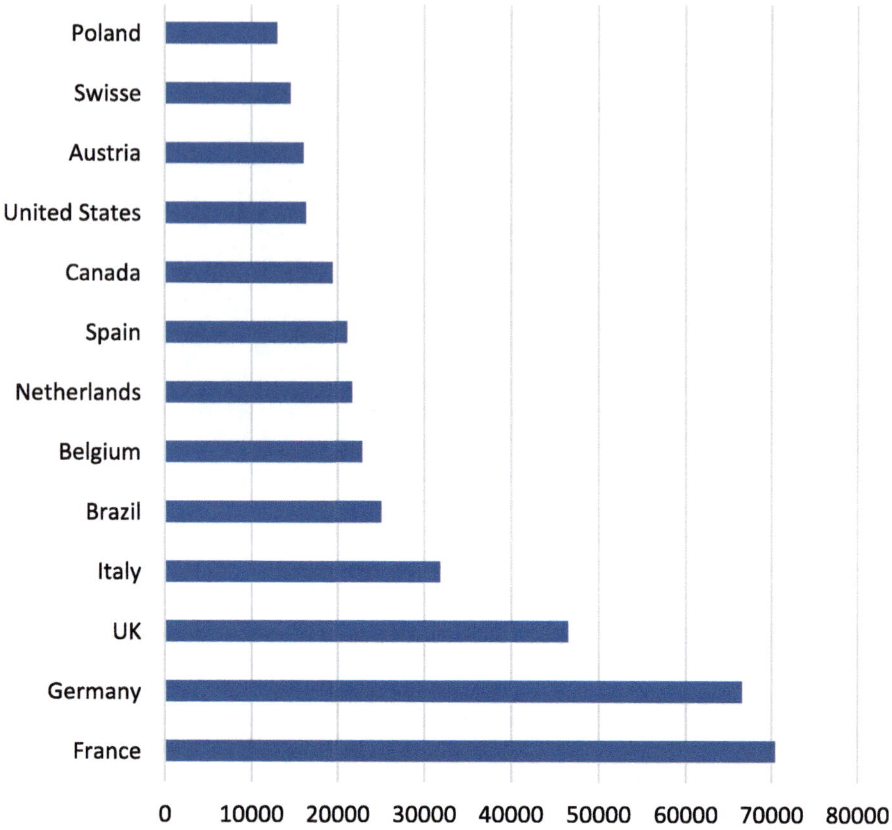

Fig. 3.2 Country of participants. Source: Author elaboration

think that by law directors should define measures and procedures to identify and possibly prevent ESG risks. On the content of the due diligence proposal, the respondents did not find an absolute majority unlike in the previous points. The majority position (about 40%) showed its preference for the European Union to define a mandatory minimum content with particular attention to environmental issues such as climate neutrality or the loss of biodiversity. Furthermore, above all companies, for fear of competitive disadvantages compared to companies belonging to other contexts and therefore not subject to European regulations, would extend the provisions on sustainable corporate governance and due diligence also to third-country companies carrying out activities in Europe even if they are not established on the mainland.

Lastly, it is also interesting to highlight the results regarding the thinking on skills that directors should have in order to be able to govern and understand human rights-related issues or ESG issues more generally. The respondents suggest introducing rules according to which some directors with expertise in ESG issues should be appointed to the boards of directors. Some have instead suggested the requirement to carry out periodic assessments of the level of competence in matters relating to the environment, social affairs, and human rights and to regularly follow the training and in-depth courses.

3.6.2 Provisions

The Directive provides obligations and responsibilities for certain types of companies, identified in Chap. 2, on issues that fall within the scope of negative impacts on human rights and environmental impacts. These areas extend from the company's activities to those of its subsidiaries and the supply chain. Article 1 speaks of companies with which "established business relationships" are maintained. The same directive specifies that this term refers to:

- With whom the company has a commercial agreement or to whom the company provides financing, insurance, or reinsurance or
- That performs business operations related to the products or services of the company for or on behalf of the company

Also of interest is the definition that the Commission adopts to circumscribe the meaning of "negative impacts." To define the negative impacts on human rights and the environment, it has included in the annex a list of violations pertaining to the social and environmental sphere on the basis of the various international conventions.

It is possible to group the structure of the Directive into four groups that group the different articles:

- (art. 1–3) Introductory provision
- (art. 4–16) Methods of application of the due diligence obligation
- (art. 17–21 and 22) Monitoring of compliance with the obligations and the sanction regime
- (art. 25) climate
- (Article 26) due diligence

3.6.3 Scope of the Obliged Subjects

Article 2 precisely defines the subjects falling within the scope of the Directive. The commission specifies within the Directive what it defines for companies by inserting an exhaustive list of cases. For simplicity, it should be noted that the Commission has decided to include both non-financial companies and financial ones. The article provides that the obligations extend to:

1. "the company had more than 500 employees on average and had a net worldwide turnover of more than EUR 150 million in the last financial year for which annual financial statements have been prepared;
2. the company did not reach the thresholds under point (a), but had more than 250 employees on average and had a net worldwide turnover of more than EUR 40 million in the last financial year for which annual financial statements have been prepared, provided that at least 50% of this net turnover was generated in one or more of the following sectors:
   (a) the manufacture of textiles, leather and related products (including footwear), and the wholesale trade of textiles, clothing and footwear;
   (b) agriculture, forestry, fisheries (including aquaculture), the manufacture of food products, and the wholesale trade of agricultural raw materials, live animals, wood, food, and beverages;
   (c) the extraction of mineral resources regardless of where they are extracted (including crude petroleum, natural gas, coal, lignite, metals and metal ores, as well as all other, non-metallic minerals and quarry products), the manufacture of basic metal products, other non-metallic mineral products and fabricated metal products (except machinery and equipment), and the wholesale trade of mineral resources, basic and intermediate mineral products (including metals and metal ores, construction materials, fuels, chemicals and other intermediate products)." (EU Commission, 2022, pp. 46–47)

The provisions of the directive, as suggested by the preliminary consultations, are also required of some types of companies not incorporated in Europe. Specifically, the legislation provides that companies established in third countries but which exceed at least one of the following limits also fall within the scope of the Directive:

- A net turnover exceeding 150 million EUR
- Turnover between 40 and 150 million in the last financial year in cases where at least half of the turnover deriving from activities in the sectors listed above (EU Commission, 2022, pp. 47)

In this first phase it appears that the SMEs do not fall within the scope of the Directive. Also on the basis of the consultations, the Commission has decided to exclude smaller companies since a more stringent regulation on due diligence would entail high costs in terms of finance, organization, and skills that SMEs could find it difficult to bear. However, it should be noted that although SMEs have been excluded from Article 2 of the Directive, the latter could affect them due to possible links with the value chain of the company subject to the Directive, including the supply chain. Therefore, the aforementioned "business relation" greatly extends the impact of the Directive on the European entrepreneurial fabric.

3.6.4 *Content of the Directive*

Article 4 provides for:

(a) "integrating due diligence into their policies;
(b) identifying actual or potential adverse impacts;
(c) preventing and mitigating potential adverse impacts, and bringing actual adverse impacts to an end and minimizing their extent;
(d) establishing and maintaining a complaints procedure;
(e) monitoring the effectiveness of their due diligence policy and measures;
(f) publicly communicating on due diligence." (EU Commission, 2022, pp. 53)

Article 5 deals with the obligation that companies have to integrate due diligence into their policies. Companies are required to define due diligence policies:

- A comprehensive overview of the company's approach to due diligence, including its long-term plans
- Define a code of conduct for the company's employees and subsidiaries
- Describing the procedures and measures put in place to ensure compliance with company policies, including verifying that these guidelines are being followed throughout all business dealings (EU Commission, 2022, pp. 54)

Regarding point b, article 6 provides that companies must identify the negative impacts, ex ante and ex-post, relating to the business activity on human rights and the environment.

The companies covered by point b) of Article 1 should only identify the impacts considered to be seriously associated with their sector. As far as financial companies are concerned, the law regulates that they should identify the negative impacts in the loan or credit disbursement process.

The European Commission emphasizes the need to identify actual and potential threats as much as it emphasizes the need to prevent potential negative impacts. The activities covered by article 7 are preparatory for an attempt to reduce any negative externalities in a preventive manner. In particular, the article provides that companies are required to:

- "were necessary due to the nature or complexity of the measures required for the prevention, develop and implement a prevention action plan, with reasonable and clearly defined timelines for action and qualitative and quantitative indicators for measuring improvement. The prevention action plan shall be developed in consultation with affected stakeholders;
- seek contractual assurances from a business partner with whom it has a direct business relationship that it will ensure compliance with the company's code of conduct and, as necessary, a prevention action plan, including by seeking corresponding contractual assurances from its partners, to the extent that their activities are part of the company's value chain (contractual cascading). When such contractual assurances are obtained, paragraph 4 shall apply;

- make necessary investments, such as into management or production processes and infrastructures, to comply with paragraph 1;
- provide targeted and proportionate support for an SME with which the company has an established business relationship, where compliance with the code of conduct or the prevention action plan would jeopardize the viability of the SME;
- in compliance with Union law including competition law, collaborate with other entities, including, where relevant, to increase the company's ability to bring the adverse impact to an end, in particular where no other action is suitable or effective" (EU Commission, 2022, pp. 55).

The Commission identifies a list of activities that provide a framework of procedures and best practices that companies need to implement to prevent negative impacts. The list above clearly shows the role assigned to large companies of supervision of the companies with which they come into contact. Specific conditions have been inserted in cases where the company relates to an SME. The companies covered by the Directive in this case have the burden of supporting any support and knowledge transfer costs to support the SMEs with which they enter into contractual relationships.

For negative impacts that have already occurred, the Commission dedicates Article 8:

- "neutralize the adverse impact or minimize its extent, including by the payment of damages to the affected persons and of financial compensation to the affected communities. The action shall be proportionate to the significance and scale of the adverse impact and to the contribution of the company's conduct to the adverse impact;
- where necessary because the adverse impact cannot be immediately brought to an end, develop and implement a corrective action plan with reasonable and clearly defined timelines for action and qualitative and quantitative indicators for measuring improvement. Where relevant, the corrective action plan shall be developed in consultation with stakeholders;
- seek contractual assurances from a direct partner with whom it has an established business relationship that it will ensure compliance with the code of conduct and, as necessary, a corrective action plan, including by seeking corresponding contractual assurances from its partners, to the extent that they are part of the value chain (contractual cascading). When such contractual assurances are obtained, paragraph 5 shall apply.
- make necessary investments, such as into management or production processes and infrastructures to comply with paragraphs 1, 2 and 3;
- provide targeted and proportionate support for an SME with which the company has an established business relationship, where compliance with the code of conduct or the corrective action plan would jeopardise the viability of the SME;
- in compliance with Union law including competition law, collaborate with other entities, including, where relevant, to increase the company's ability to bring the adverse impact to an end, in particular where no other action is suitable or effective" (EU Commission, 2022, pp. 56–57).

Furthermore, the subjects who can present a complaint if they have a reasonable doubt of any negative impact on the matters covered by the Directive are identified. The European regulator has provided that any person affected by a negative impact, from trade unions or other representatives of workers operating along the value chain, civil society organizations in sectors connected to the value chain have the legitimacy to complain. The company must follow up on the complaint received and meet the representatives of the person or persons who have complained.

Finally, points e) and f) are described in articles 10 and 11. Art. 10 regulates the monitoring activity that the company independently must carry out periodically regarding the activities explained in the previous points for the entire value chain. Therefore, companies must equip themselves with a system of qualitative and quantitative key performance indicators (KPIs) controls from which to discern an assessment at least annually. The social performance control system is the basis for making considerations and assessments and possibly updating the due diligence policy.

According to the art. 11, companies must publish a statement by 30 April of each financial year to be published on the company institutional website.

3.6.5 External Monitoring and Sanctions

The Member State must guarantee external control in order to supervise compliance with the due diligence legislation. Each state can designate one or more supervisory authorities who have the task of supervising the application of the new rules and, in the event of non-application, sanctioning non-compliant companies. The national authorities are also responsible for supervising companies from third countries which have a branch in the state or, if the company does not have one, which has generated the highest percentage of turnover in the territory of the state.

The powers of the national supervisory authority include the possibility of carrying out investigations ex officio and carrying out inspections, in compliance with national laws, where it deems it needs further information. Furthermore, the authority can:

- "to order the cessation of infringements of the national provisions adopted according to this Directive, abstention from any repetition of the relevant conduct and, where appropriate, remedial action proportionate to the infringement and necessary to bring it to an end;
- to impose pecuniary sanctions;
- to adopt interim measures to avoid the risk of severe and irreparable harm" (EU Commission, 2022, pp. 62).

Concerning the sanctions, the Commission states that they will be quantified based on the turnover of the non-compliant company. At the European level, the Commission sets up a European network of supervisors that will bring together representatives of national bodies. This measure is aimed at ensuring the coordination of regulatory practices in the various Member States.

Articles 25 and 26 are addressed to the directors. Directors should "take into account the consequences of their decisions for sustainability matters, including, where applicable, human rights, climate change, and environmental consequences, including in the short, medium and long term." Directors are also responsible for preparing due diligence actions and for supervising them.

3.7 Final Comments

The proposal for a Directive on Due Diligence falls within the regulatory interventions desired by the European Commission about Sustainable Corporate Governance. The results of the widely participated consultation show how well such a proposal is welcomed by the different groups of stakeholders. They unanimously expressed the need for a regulatory intervention aimed at increasing the responsibility of companies in matters of sustainability.

The proposed directive seeks to align with the best practices identified by international frameworks such as the one issued by the OECD, UN Guiding Principles on Business and Human Rights as well as the ILO. In fact, the proposal tries to follow the approach present in the OECD document (OECD, 2018). The same configuration of the articles follows the phases present in the following figure (Fig. 3.3).

Articles 5 to 11 retrace the stages of a due diligence process. Starting from the introduction of responsibility for environmental and human rights issues in corporate policies (provided for in Article 5), the subsequent phases concern: assessing negative impacts (Article 6), mitigating or preventing any (art. 7), control (art. 10) and finally communication (art. 11).

It is interesting to find within the legislation an attempt to give definitions to some terms and areas. A problem that has been highlighted in the literature is, for example, the definition of risk and impact and in particular of impact in terms of human rights. If you do not understand what and which aspects generate a negative impact on human rights risks, the due diligence process cannot be implemented effectively (Björn Fasterling, 2017). Therefore, a definition of what is meant by adverse environmental and human rights impacts is to be welcomed.

The articles included in the proposal require companies to make significant efforts to implement a system of internal procedures aimed at preventing or mitigating negative impacts. Therefore, the commitment that European companies should make mustn't reduce the competitive capacity of the European entrepreneurial fabric compared to those who would be exempt from these obligations. Europe must guarantee itself in maintaining the competitiveness of companies internally and externally. About the first point, the proposal provides a wide margin to individual nations in transposing the Directive into national legislation. This could lead to significant differences between member countries which would influence the

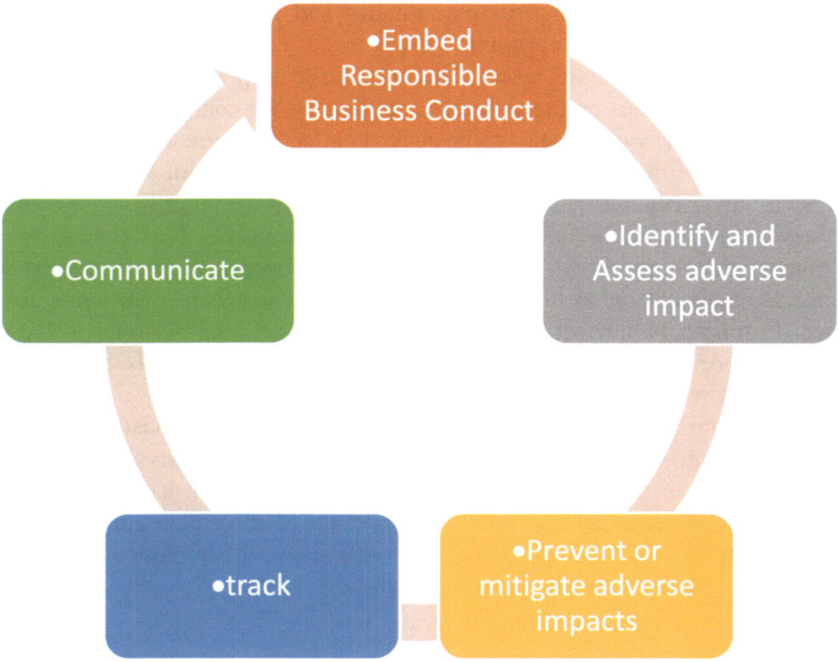

Fig. 3.3 Due diligence process

behavior of resident companies. The adoption of more stringent legislation would compromise the competitiveness of companies that will have to compete in the competitive scenario with other organizations relieved of regulatory commitments. A similar discourse recurs in external competition. The extension of the scope of the proposal also to third-party companies appears to be favorable both for extending good practices to an increasing number of entities and for safeguarding European companies.

Furthermore, as highlighted in the previous paragraph, in article 2 in which the organizations which are required to implement due diligence processes are classified, SMEs are not present. Nonetheless, SMEs may be affected due to the links some have with large companies. Furthermore, they may be subject to contractual penalties with the larger companies with which a business relationship is established. Public support and the role of larger firms in leading smaller firms will be key, although this may prove to be an additional cost to organizations. Knowledge transfer would enrich the skills of smaller firms and generate greater social value.

In this regard, there is a proposition of the proposal that is too tied to an approach with a strong system of sanctions for those who transgress the law. This could focus companies on the obligation to comply with the standard for fear of legal and financial repercussions when, otherwise, organizations should be made aware of the relevance of adopting sustainability-oriented approaches. The proposal should encourage virtuous behaviors because there is awareness of businesses and governance of the value of proactive attitudes and policies for the benefit of a sustainable transition of the economic system.

Again, the external control system identified in the proposal must be a third party with supervisory duties on the practices activated by the company. Some scholars argued that the only variables that can concretely affect the correct application of due diligence are the morality of management or regulation (Björn Fasterling, 2017; Boersma, 2018; Buhmann, 2018). The new rule could therefore increase concrete business practices and discourage phenomena of pure form.

Finally, the addition of a reference to directors intends to reiterate what was identified in the resolution of 17 December 2020 on sustainable corporate governance (European Parliament, 2020). In fact, Article 25 does not refer to the due diligence process but to the due diligence itself. The proposal extends the liability of directors who must act according to the criteria of due diligence.

However, no specific description of the obligations that administrations should comply with is given. The wording of the article, therefore, remains vague and could leave directors uncertain in the performance of their duties. This lack of detail could refer to the individual company law regulation of the Member State and could create differences in the application of the rule. In this sense, the introduction of Article 25 could be seen as an attempt at harmonization.

References

AFEP and Medef. (2020). *Corporate governance code of listing corporations*. https://www.alstom.com/sites/alstom.com/files/2020/03/27/Afep-Medef%20Code%20VUK%20Jan.%202020.pdf

Assonime. (2021). *Doveri degli amministratori e sostenibilità*. https://www.infoparlamento.it/Pdf/ShowPdf/8218

Beretta, S., & Bozzolan, S. (2008). Quality versus quantity: The case of forward-looking disclosure. *Journal of Accounting, Auditing and Finance, 23*(3), 333–375.

Boersma, M. (2018). Between norms and practice: Civil society perspectives on the legitimacy of multistakeholder initiatives to eliminate child labor. *Business Strategy and the Environment, 27*(5), 612–620. https://doi.org/10.1002/bse.2066

Bosetti, L. (2017). *La corporate governance nell'Unione europea: interventi di armonizzazione e best practices*. Giappichelli.

Buhmann, K. (2018). Neglecting the proactive aspect of human rights due diligence? A critical appraisal of the EU's non-financial reporting directive as a pillar one avenue for promoting pillar two action. *Business and Human Rights Journal, 3*(1), 23–45.

Cadbury, A. (1992). *Report of the committee on the financial aspects of corporate governance*. Gee & Co.

Cinquini, L., Passetti, E., Tenucci, A., & Frey, M. (2012). Analyzing intellectual capital information in sustainability reports: Some empirical evidence. *Journal of Intellectual Capital, 13*(4), 531–561.

Comision Nacional del Mercado de Valores. (2020). *Good governance code of listed companies*. https://www.cnmv.es/DocPortal/Publicaciones/CodigoGov/CBG_2020_ENen.PDF

Comitato Corporate Governance. (2020). *Codice di Corporate Governance*. https://www.borsaitaliana.it/comitato-corporate-governance/codice/2020.pdf

Denedo, M., Thomson, I., & Yonekura, A. (2017). International advocacy NGOs, counter accounting, accountability and engagement. *Accounting Auditing & Accountability Journal, 30*(6, SI), 1309–1343.

Denedo, M., Thomson, I., & Yonekura, A. (2019). Ecological damage, human rights and oil: Local advocacy NGOs dialogic action and alternative accounting practices. *Accounting Forum, 43*(1, SI), 85–112.

Doni, F., Bianchi Martini, S., Corvino, A., & Mazzoni, M. (2019). Voluntary versus mandatory non-financial disclosure. *Meditari Accountancy Research, 28*(5), 781–802. https://doi.org/10.1108/medar-12-2018-0423

Ernst and Young. (2020). *Study on directors' duties and sustainable corporate governance.* Report prepared by EY for the European Commission DG Justice and Consumers. https://op.europa.eu/en/publication-detail/-/publication/e47928a2-d20b-11ea-adf7-01aa75ed71a1/language-en.

EU Commission. (2018). *Action plan: Financing sustainable growth.* https://eur-lex.europa.eu/legal-content/EN/TXT/?uri=CELEX%3A52018DC0097

EU Commission. (2020a). *Inception impact assessment 'sustainable corporate governance'.* Ref. Ares(2020)4034032 – 30/07/2020. https://ec.europa.eu/info/law/betterregulation/have-your-say/initiatives/12548-Sustainable-corporate-governance.

EU Commission. (2020b). *Summary report of the public consultation on the review of the non-financial reporting directive.* Ref. Ares(2020)3997889 – 29/07/2020. https://eur-lex.europa.eu/legal-content/EN/TXT/?uri5pi_com%3AAres%282020%293997889

EU Commission. (2021). *Proposal for a Directive of the European parliament and of the council amending Directive 2013/34/EU, Directive 2004/109/EC, Directive 2006/43/EC and Regulation (EU) No 537/2014, as regards corporate sustainability reporting.* https://eur-lex.europa.eu/legal-content/EN/TXT/?uri5CELEX%3A52021PC0189

EU Commission. (2022). *Proposal for a Directive of the European parliament and of the council on corporate sustainability due diligence and amending Directive (EU) 2019/1937.* https://eur-lex.europa.eu/legal-content/EN/TXT/?uri=CELEX%3A52022PC0071

European Parliament. (2020, December 17). *Resolution of 17 December 2020 on sustainable corporate governance.* https://www.europarl.europa.eu/doceo/document/TA-9-2020-0372_EN.html

Fasterling, B. (2017). Human rights due diligence as risk management: Social risk versus human rights risk. *Business and Human Rights Journal, 2*(2), 225–247. https://doi.org/10.1017/BHJ.2016.26

Financial Reporting Council. (2018). *The UK corporate governance code.* https://www.frc.org.uk/getattachment/88bd8c45-50ea-4841-95b0-d2f4f48069a2/2018-UK-Corporate-Governance-Code-FINAL.PDF

La Torre, M., Sabelfeld, S., Blomkvist, M., & Dumay, J. (2020). Rebuilding trust: Sustainability and non-financial reporting and the European Union regulation. *Meditari Accountancy Research, 28*(August), 701–725.

Mio, C., Marchini, P. L., & Medioli, A. (2020). Forward-looking information in integrated reports: Insights from "best in class". *Corporate Social Responsibility and Environmental Management.* csr.1959.

Muserra, A. L., Papa, M., & Grimaldi, F. (2020). Sustainable development and the European Union policy on non-financial information: An Italian empirical analysis. *Corporate Social Responsibility and Environmental Management, 27*(1), 22–31.

OECD. (2018). *Due diligence guidance for responsible business conduct.*

Paolone, F., Granà, F., Martiniello, L., & Tiscini, R. (2021). Environmental risk indicators disclosure and value relevance: An empirical analysis of Italian listed companies after the implementation of the Legislative Decree 254/2016. *Corporate Social Responsibility and Environmental Management, 28*(5), 1471–1482.

Stacchezzini, R., Melloni, G., & Lai, A. (2016). Sustainability management and reporting: The role of integrated reporting for communicating corporate sustainability management. *Journal of Cleaner Production, 136*, 102–110.

Veltri, S., De Luca, F., & Phan, H. (2020). Do investors value companies' mandatory nonfinancial risk disclosure? An empirical analysis of the Italian context after the EU directive. *Business Strategy and the Environment, 29*(6), 2226–2237.

Venturelli, A., Pizzi, S., Caputo, F., & Principale, S. (2020). The revision of nonfinancial reporting directive: A critical lens on the comparability principle. *Business Strategy and the Environment, 29*(8), 3584–3597. https://doi.org/10.1002/bse.2598

Zattoni, A. (2020). *Corporate governance*. Egea.

Chapter 4
Human Rights Due Diligence and Corporate Governance: A European Analysis

Keywords Human rights · Human rights due diligence · Corporate governance · CSR committee · Sustainable corporate governance

4.1 Introduction

Human rights represent the most relevant area within the S dimension of the environmental, social, and governance triad. Human rights have become even more relevant when contextualized in the current period where the COVID-19 pandemic has aggravated the relevance of social issues (Paoloni et al., 2023). Regardless of the sector of activity, human rights have the distinction of being an issue that affects all global companies. Sectoral differences appear to be crucial in terms of the weight and relevance of the topic but they do not exempt any company from not considering it as a material issue. Companies must guarantee respect for human rights in the relationships established within the system, of all personnel who operate within the company, and externally, in the relationships established by the company with the various subjects. This theme becomes even more relevant for large European companies in the light of the regulatory intentions of the European Commission. The Due Diligence proposal formulated in this way would require companies to make significant organizational efforts to modify their processes in line with the Directive. Therefore, it is necessary that European companies are ready for probable new legislation of the European Commission and begin to approach the new matter. The objective of the research is therefore to evaluate the state of the art of due diligence practices of European companies and to evaluate the governance determinants that may have influenced good practices in the field of human rights.

S. Principale, *Fostering Sustainability in Corporate Governance*, SIDREA Series in Accounting and Business Administration,
https://doi.org/10.1007/978-3-031-30354-8_4

4.2 Human Rights-Related Disclosure

1948 was the year in which the United Nations (UN) issued the Universal Declaration on Human Rights, sanctioning the inviolable rights of human beings. On the basis of this fundamental document, some organizations have tried to formulate guidelines for all companies as systems also composed of a human component (Bertini, 1990; Onida, 1971).

The Guiding Principles had the task of providing initial indications on how companies can rethink their way of doing business, giving importance to corporate social responsibility and the fundamental protection of human rights (UN, 2018). These guidelines put respect for human rights first and also set out the methods and procedures that companies should follow to manage human rights risks (Antonini et al., 2020). Furthermore, the Guiding Principles also introduce the relevance of defining and implementing due diligence procedures as a tool for internal and external assurance.

Following the introduction of the Principles on Human Rights and in general the spread of the non-financial reporting tool, the attention of accounting scholars on the subject has also increased. Recent studies have analyzed human rights-related disclosure on the basis of the principles and guidelines of the Global Reporting Initiative (GRI) which also provides an appropriate basis for reporting on social information (Hazelton, 2013). Studies have found that companies have low transparency in reporting human rights information (Parsa et al., 2018; Ullah et al., 2021). In this regard, the regulation has produced positive effects on human rights-related disclosure. Some NFRD scholars argue that the Directive has increased the amount of information about human rights (Leopizzi et al., 2020; Matuszak & Różańska, 2021). Although the data cannot be considered satisfactory, the Directive has shed light on areas often overlooked by companies.

However, there are several critical positions in the literature regarding the disclosure of human rights by accounting scholars (Alarcón & Cole, 2019; Kreander & McPhail, 2019; Lauwo & Otusanya, 2014; Ullah et al., 2021; Zeng et al., 2022; Pianezzi et al., 2022). The authors, on the one hand, argue that human rights accounting is only at an initial stage. The gap should be filled above all by theoretical contributions that can better define the relationship between human rights and corporate activities (McPhail et al., 2016; McPhail & Ferguson, 2016). On the other hand, they criticize the difficulty of accounting and non-financial reporting in being able to really highlight any bad working conditions or potential violations of human rights. Studies conducted in developing countries as well as contributions analyzing multinational companies have found evidence of the limitations of reporting on human rights issues (Kun, 2018; Lauwo & Otusanya, 2014; van der Ploeg & Vanclay, 2017). Indeed, the reporting tool is a tool to legitimize the activities carried out. Furthermore, the use of graphic methods of impression management is widespread among companies that want to disseminate news related to human rights (Zeng et al., 2022).

4.2.1 Human Rights Due Diligence

Corporate responsibility regarding respect for human rights has relevant implications for corporate governance. The human rights principles treat respect for human rights in the business context as a process of management, governance, and communication (UN, 2018). It has been emphasized from many quarters that corporate governance is not capable of understanding the extension of relevant issues also to social areas such as human rights (Karin Buhmann et al., 2019; Byrne & Lee Ludvigsen, 2022).

Human Rights Principles have developed a framework for businesses to respect human rights. Human rights accountability has been declined according to a due diligence approach.

The term Due Diligence is referred to generically as "a process of discovery that is relevant in key business transactions as well as operational activities" (Spedding, 2005). In a typical financial environment, they are functional activities and recognize any responsibilities and evaluate the integrity of information. From being a typical financial process, with the publication of the "Guiding Principles on Business and Human Rights" (Principles) it was also extended to areas that differ from commercial risk. The rationale is identified in stimulating companies to be accountable for these issues.

According to the guiding principles of the United Nations, human rights due diligence is expressed in the identification, prevention, mitigation, and accounting of impacts on human rights. The definition of the due diligence process thus exposed would seem to bring these activities closer to those commonly carried out for risk management. However, the main objective of a human rights due diligence process is to prevent the risks of a lack of respect for human rights rather than correcting any violations ex post (Fasterling, 2017).

Properly performed due diligence should become the preparatory phase for a responsible decision (Fasterling & Demuijnck, 2013). However, it should be considered that any due diligence process carried out correctly and scrupulously has the limit of being an activity that requires the use and consumption of various resources. This, according to the literature on the subject, could represent a strong criticality.

Companies that decide to carry out activities to prevent, mitigate, and disclose human rights risks, in the presence of the high costs of due diligence activities, run the risk of focusing on the substance rather than on the substantial activities. There may be episodes in which companies, as happened for ESG information in general (Mahoney et al., 2013; Wang & Sarkis, 2017; Munasinghe et al., 2021) communicate and describe the due diligence system that does not proportionally substantiate in concrete efforts. Furthermore, also on the disclosure side, companies could be discouraged from a transparent disclosure of the risks and impacts on human rights. Any negative impacts or transgressions could be used against the company and above all not be appreciated by the various stakeholders. The information could be used as third-party evidence in litigation against the company (Sherman & Lehr, 2010).

To overcome these critical issues, scholars argue that proper human rights due diligence cannot fail to be associated with a contextual moral commitment by managers (Muchlinski, 2012; Fasterling & Demuijnck, 2013). Moral commitment would be the only driver, in the absence of external regulation, so that a concrete commitment to evaluate and mitigate the impacts on human rights can be achieved which is substantial and not superficial (Björn Fasterling, 2017).

4.3 Research Aim

Based on the foregoing, the research conducted intends to carry out exploratory research focused on the last part of the due diligence process: communication. The objective of the investigation is twofold. The first objective is to carry out an initial mapping of the companies that have decided to voluntarily implement a human rights due diligence process to assess the degree of attention of European companies to social issues. The investigation is aimed at understanding the state of the art of the companies which, according to the proposed Directive, could be involved. The second has the purpose of evaluating whether some governance mechanisms can contribute to encouraging proactive actions to respect human rights. The literature and international frameworks presented in the previous paragraphs underline the direct link between corporate governance and human rights due diligence.

4.4 Methods

4.4.1 Sample

The sample consists of European Public Interest Entities (PIEs). These companies all fall within the scope of the obligations of Directive 95/2014/EU on non-financial reporting. The decision to analyze these types of companies is due to their now 5-year experience in dealing with ESG issues in compliance with the provisions of the NFRD. Furthermore, due to regulatory obligations (Directive 2014/95/EU) companies are required to communicate external information on how respect for human rights is integrated into the business model and various company processes.

The sample was defined using the Amadeus Bureau van Dijk database. This database contains a large amount of information about European companies. Financial and insurance companies were excluded from the sample. These types of companies are subject to greater regulation than non-financial companies and therefore their inclusion in the sample could compromise the homogeneity of the same. The final sample of companies is therefore made up of 813 units. Table 4.1 shows the composition of the sample by sector.

Table 4.1 Sample description

Accommodation and food services	12
Construction	58
Health care and social assistance	24
Information	88
Manufacturing	354
Mining, quarrying, and oil and gas extraction	40
Professional, scientific, and technical services	35
Real estate	46
Retail trade	46
Transportation and warehousing	57
Utilities	33
Wholesale trade	20

4.4.2 Methodology

Mixed methods have been adopted for the analysis of the due diligence and of the internal factors of the company which may have influenced the treatment. The use of qualitative and quantitative methodologies is useful in order to overcome the limits deriving from the single use of one method rather than the other.

As far as the qualitative part is concerned, a content analysis was used. The use of this method is used by various scholars in the literature for the textual analysis of documents (Krippendorff, 2018). Through the textual analysis of the non-financial statements of the European PIEs it was possible to evaluate the companies that reported that they had implemented human rights due diligence processes. The coding activities were carried out on the non-financial statements European companies in 2021.

Subsequently, a logistic regression analysis was performed to evaluate the internal factors that influenced the adoption of good practices in terms of human rights due diligence. This method belongs to the quantitative tools and makes it possible to evaluate whether the variables considered in the model have a significant relationship with the variable being analyzed.

4.4.3 Variables

By adopting a logistic regression, the dependent variable is a dichotomous variable, i.e. one that has values of 0 or 1. Therefore, the dependent variable has a value of 1 if the company describes the due diligence procedures adopted while it has a value of 0 if there are no information about the practices adopted. The disclosure of information about human rights due diligence can be considered as a proxy for the policy adopted.

To evaluate the influence of governance mechanisms on the due diligence policy, the most widely used variables in the literature have been identified. In particular, to

Table 4.2 Variables

Variables	Measure	Ab.
Human rights due diligence	If the due diligence procedure described 1, otherwise 0	HRDD
Size	Logarithm of the total asset	Lnasset
Leverage	Leverage	LEV
Return of assets	Net income on total assets	ROA
Book market value	Total assets minus total liabilities	bv
Esg performance	Asset 4 ESG Score (0–100)	ESG_P
Number of the board	Number of directors on the board	BoardSize
Female directors	Percentage of female directors	F_B
Independent directors	Percentage of independent directors	I_B
CSR committee	Presence of a CSR committee 1, 0 otherwise	CSR_C
CEO duality	Office of president and CEO entrusted to the same person	CEO_D

measure the governance mechanisms, the number of directors who make up the board of directors, the percentage of female directors, the percentage of independent directors, the presence of a CSR committee, and the CEO Duality (if the CEO covers also the position of chairman of the board of directors).

Finally, following the practice identified in the literature, some control measures were included in the model. Variables have been included that measure company size and economic-financial and ESG performance. The logarithm of total assets was used as the dimensional variable. ROA (return on assets) and leverage were instead included in the model as performance indicators. The ESG performance variable measures the social, environmental, and governance performance of companies. This indicator is a measure made up of various items and is used in various scientific works to measure the ESG results obtained by companies (Table 4.2).

4.5 Results

Table 4.3 reports the descriptive statistics of the variables used in the empirical model. The dependent variable HRDD is disclosed on average by 13.9% of the sample. The data, therefore, highlights that only less than a seventh of the companies obliged to deal with human rights issues have implemented a human rights due diligence policy system. With regard to the independent variables, the boards are made up of an average number of about ten people with a standard deviation of almost four members. Analyzing the gender variable, less than 30% of the boards of European companies are made up of female directors (standard deviation of 12.54). Instead, about 70% of companies have set up a CSR committee internally. Finally, only in 18% of cases the CEO also has the position of chairman of the board.

Table 4.3 Descriptive statistics

Variable	Obs	Mean	Std. dev.	Min	Max
HRDD	813	0.139	0.346	0	1
Lnasset	812	22,811	1803	18.032	28.57
LEV	812	0.391	0.251	−1.011	1
ROA	809	0.048	0.115	−0.674	2368
bv	809	63,261	1179.538	−34,661	33,471.626
ESG_P	813	90.357	23.065	1515	100
BoardSize	813	10,635	3886	2	23
F_B	813	28,616	12.54	0	71,429
I_B	812	60,686	22,747	0	100
CSR_C	813	0.695	0.461	0	1
CEO_D	813	0.18	0.384	0	1

Table 4.4 Percentage by countries

Country	Companies	Percentage
Austria	2	0.133333
Belgium	3	0.12
Czech Republic	0	0
Denmark	4	0.148148
Finland	4	0.166667
France	19	0.215909
Germany	16	0.183908
Hungary	1	0.25
Republic of Ireland	0	0
Italy	5	0.125
Luxembourg	0	0
Netherlands	3	0.096774
Norway	0	0
Poland	0	0
Portugal	1	0.111111
Spain	12	0.292683
Sweden	6	0.111111
United Kingdom	37	0.122112

From an analysis by country, the nation with the highest percentage of companies that have activated virtuous human rights due diligence processes is Spain (29%). Following are France (21%) and Germany (18%) (Table 4.4).

The following Table 4.5 instead shows the results of the due diligence by business sector. The sectors with a higher percentage of companies that have described and implemented a due diligence system are Utilities (33%), Retail (24%), and Manufacturing (22%).

Before carrying out the regression analyses, a correlation analysis had to be carried out first. The analysis is necessary to evaluate ex ante the potential presence of high correlations that could be an expression of multicollinearity phenomena. The

Table 4.5 Percentage by sectors

Sectors	Companies	Percentage
Accommodation and food services	1	8
Construction	6	16
Health care and social assistance	1	20
Information	9	14
Manufacturing	56	22
Mining, quarrying, and oil and gas extraction	4	10
Professional, scientific, and technical services	5	14
Real estate and rental and leasing	1	2
Retail trade	11	24
Transportation and warehousing	6	16
Utilities	11	33
Wholesale trade	2	10

results of Table 4.6 exclude the possibility of the presence of similar phenomena. From the analysis of the coefficients it is possible to evaluate how there is a positive correlation between the dependent variable and the governance mechanisms considered. Particular is the negative correlation between the disclosure of due diligence processes and ESG performance.

Table 4.7 instead shows the results of the logistic regression. Six different models were performed to evaluate the influence of the different governance mechanisms individually (1–5) and overall in the model 6.

Model 1 detects the positive and significant relationship between the dependent variable and board size ($\beta = 0.218$, $p < 0.05$). Model 2 shows that the gender variable positively influences the dependent variable ($\beta = 0.0132$, $p < 0.1$). Model 3 does not show any significant relationship between the employee variable and the percentage of independent directors. Conversely, model 4 shows that there is a positive and significant relationship between human rights due diligence and the presence of a CSR committee ($\beta = 0.813$, $p < 0.01$). Similarly, in model 5 the variable Ceo duality positively influences the dependent variable ($\beta = 0.686$, $p < 0.01$). Finally, model 6 shows the overall results of the different governance mechanisms. In particular, it is possible to observe how the variables Board Size ($\beta = 0.0833$, $p < 0.10$), Csr Committee ($\beta = 0.733$, $p < 0.05$), and Ceo Duality ($\beta = 0.537$, $p < 0.05$) positively influence the dependent variable. There are no significant relationships of Due Diligence with the gender variable. Concerning the control variables, it is possible to observe how the company size is a significant variable in all the models considered and produces a positive influence. Particular is the result of a discrepancy between CSR performance and the adoption of due diligence practices. Although weak, negative relationships were found in the models shown in the table.

Table 4.6 Matrix of correlations

Variables	(1)	(2)	(3)	(4)	(5)	(6)	(7)	(8)	(9)	(10)	(11)
(1) Hm	1000										
(2) lnasset	0.193	1000									
(3) Lev	−0.035	−0.403	1000								
(4) ROA	0.024	−0.151	0.117	1000							
(5) B.V	−0.014	−0.042	−0.000	−0.067	1000						
(6) ESG_P	−0.189	−0.366	0.139	0.045	0.011	1000					
(7) B_Size	0.184	0.556	−0.304	−0.083	0.016	−0.194	1000				
(8) F_B	0.090	0.264	−0.144	0.002	−0.012	−0.046	0.183	1000			
(9) I_B	0.015	0.056	0.109	−0.008	−0.091	−0.076	−0.243	0.138	1000		
(10) CSR_C	0.143	0.284	−0.191	−0.013	0.028	−0.188	0.216	0.109	0.032	1000	
(11) CEO_D	0.108	0.110	−0.086	−0.017	−0.015	−0.012	0.200	0.125	−0.154	0.095	1000

Table 4.7 Logit regression models

	(1)	(2)	(3)	(4)	(5)	(6)
	HRDD	HRDD	HRDD	HRDD	HRDD	HRDD
HRDD						
lnasset	0.218** (2.67)	0.280*** (3.71)	0.304*** (4.09)	0.271*** (3.63)	0.297*** (3.93)	0.175* (2.03)
LEV	1030 (1.91)	0.840 (1.62)	0.848 (1.63)	0.957 (1.80)	0.900 (1.72)	1206* (2.13)
ROA	1.414 (1.79)	1334 (1.69)	1.418 (1.80)	1475 (1.81)	1453 (1.83)	1461 (1.79)
bv	−0.00302 (−0.86)	−0.00174 (−0.63)	−0.00165 (−0.63)	−0.00174 (−0.67)	−0.00243 (−0.74)	−0.00424 (−1.12)
ESGsore	−0.0118** (−2.97)	−0.0118** (−2.97)	−0.0116** (−2.93)	−0.0103** (−2.60)	−0.0122** (−3.07)	−0.0115** (−2.83)
BoardSize	0.0900** (2.97)					0.0833* (2.51)
GenderD		0.0132* (1.45)				0.00944 (0.99)
Ind			−0.00203 (−0.43)			0.00301 (0.57)
CSRComm				0.813** (2.74)		0.733** (2.44)
CEODuality					0.686** (2.82)	0.537** (2.10)
_cons	−7.252*** (−3.51)	−8.037*** (−4.03)	−8100*** (−4.09)	−8.242*** (−4.14)	−8.152*** (−4.06)	−7.422*** (−3.53)
No	809	809	809	809	809	809
R^2	0.242	0.242	0.244	0.245	0.242	0.244
adj. R^2	0.210	0.211	0.212	0.211	0.212	0.212

*** $p<0.01$, ** $p<0.05$, * $p<0.1$

4.6 Discussion of the Results

The analysis carried out highlights not very encouraging results regarding the due diligence of human rights. European companies are reluctant to disclose human rights due diligence procedures. Empirical evidence showed that around one-eighth of the firms in the sample disclosed a description of their human rights due diligence procedures in their non-financial disclosure. This is an atypical figure if we consider the disclosure obligations to which the companies analyzed are subject. The NFRS planned to disclose the scope of the due diligence concerning the five sustainable issues, which also included human rights.

From the analysis by country, it is possible to see how there is variability, albeit not too high, between the different nations. The result regarding France and Germany is unexpected. In view of the national codes on corporate governance, it was conceivable to expect better results from companies operating in those member states. Above all, the case of Germany is anomalous since it has provided for a due diligence system regarding the supply network and on which respect for human rights is a very relevant and relevant issue. The data could therefore suggest the little relevance of national governance codes and governance models adopted by companies. Several studies have highlighted how much the different characteristics of the different contexts in which companies could influence the strategic management (Gallego-Álvarez & Ortas, 2017). The European regulator should reflect on considering adjusting in view of the context in which the company operates. Studies have, for example, highlighted how much cultural factors can greatly affect the behavior of the company (Le Luo & Tang, 2016; Panfilo & Krasodomska, 2022; Pizzi et al., 2022a, b; Sannino et al., 2020).

The sectoral analysis does not highlight any virtuous sector. The utility sector is more represented with 33% of companies that provided the information to the public. Sectors with a high human rights impact, likewise, did not stand out from the others. For example, only 10% of mining companies provided a set of information useful for evaluating processes for mitigating and preventing negative impacts on human rights. These results are unexpected as there is various evidence in the literature of the criticality of the sector in ESG practices and communication. As academics have argued for the sector's relevance to environmental issues, the social issue may differ from the E dimension findings (Bhatia & Makkar, 2020; Liu & Yang, 2018). As already highlighted, the social and human rights field concerns all companies regardless of the sector they belong to.

About the results of the logistic regression, the results show how some governance mechanisms represent positive levers in terms of human rights due diligence. The presence of a CSR Committee and the division of the office between the chairman and the CEO are the two variables that most influence the likelihood that the company adopts human rights due diligence procedures. Both results agree with the literature on the topic. As also highlighted in the previous chapter, there is various evidence of the impact of the CSR committee on CSR practices and communication (Mallin & Michelon, 2011; Vigneau et al., 2015; Cosma et al.,

2022; Pizzi et al., 2022a, b). Furthermore, the growing regulation in the ESG area as well as the need to integrate issues into the corporate system is making the CSR committee an increasingly widespread and crucial governance tool for better managing the changes underway. Furthermore, the company that decides to set up a CSR committee gives an external signal of attention to ESG issues (Helfaya & Moussa, 2017). On the other hand, the results advise against attributing two apical roles such as chairman of the board and CEO to the same figure. Part of the literature argues that the separation of roles ensures better control over management performance and a greater balance between functions (Veprauskaite & Adams, 2013; Muttakin et al., 2018). More power in the hands of a single person can lead to more neglect of stakeholder interests and indifference to CSR practices (de Villiers et al., 2011). Thus, the separation of duties increases the likelihood that the board will promote investments with potential social and environmental benefits, including human rights.

On the other hand, the influence of gender diversity on the board is slight. Although model 2 showed a weak positive correlation, this was not repeated in model 6. Therefore, it is not possible to consider gender as a significant variable in terms of due diligence (Paoloni et al., 2023). The contribution of the independent directors is also not significant.

However, the evidence needs to be corroborated and improved by further studies that can overcome the limitations of this research. The study analyzes the impact of certain governance characteristics on human rights due diligence systems over a single year. Future studies could carry out research over several years and analyze the evolution assumed by the phenomenon. In addition, future studies could analyze different drivers with respect to the characteristics of the governance structure. An area as new and delicate as that of human rights could be influenced by other factors more properly linked to the sensitivity of managers or strategic management (Galeotti, 2006). It is also interesting to evaluate the effects of the introduction of regulations on sustainable corporate governance in the light of the results of this book.

References

Alarcón, D. M., & Cole, S. (2019). No sustainability for tourism without gender equality. *Journal of Sustainable Tourism, 27*(7), 903–919.

Antonini, C., Beck, C., & Larrinaga, C. (2020). Subpolitics and sustainability reporting boundaries. The case of working conditions in global supply chains. *Accounting, Auditing & Accountability Journal, 33*(7), 1535–1567.

Bertini, U. (1990). Il sistema d'azienda : schema di analisi. In *Studi di economia e politica aziendale*. Giappichelli.

Bhatia, A., & Makkar, B. (2020). Stage of development of a country and CSR disclosure – The latent driving forces. *International Journal of Law and Management, 62*(5), 467–493.

Buhmann, K., Jonsson, J., & Fisker, M. (2019). Do no harm and do more good too: Connecting the SDGs with business and human rights and political CSR theory. *Corporate Governance (Bingley), 19*(3), 389–403.

Byrne, S., & Lee Ludvigsen, J. A. (2022). Sport mega-event governance and human rights: The 'Ruggie principles', responsibility and directions. *Leisure Studies*.

Cosma, S., Principale, S., & Venturelli, A. (2022). Sustainable governance and climate-change disclosure in European banking: The role of the corporate social responsibility committee. *Corporate Governance (Bingley), 22*(6), 1345–1369.

de Villiers, C., Naiker, V., & van Staden, C. J. (2011). The effect of board characteristics on firm environmental performance. *Journal of Management, 37*(6), 1636–1663.

Fasterling, B. (2017). Human rights due diligence as risk management: Social risk versus human rights risk. *Business and Human Rights Journal, 2*(2), 225–247.

Fasterling, B., & Demuijnck, G. (2013). Human rights in the void? Due diligence in the UN guiding principles on business and human rights. *Journal of Business Ethics, 116*(4), 799–814.

Galeotti, M. (2006). *Governo dell'azienda e indicatori di performance*. Giappichelli Editore.

Gallego-Álvarez, P. I., & Ortas, P. E. (2017). Corporate environmental sustainability reporting in the context of national cultures: A quantile regression approach. *International Business Review, 26*(2), 337–353.

Hazelton, J. (2013). Accounting as a human right: The case of water information. *Accounting, Auditing & Accountability Journal, 26*(2), 267–311.

Helfaya, A., & Moussa, T. (2017). Do board's corporate social responsibility strategy and orientation influence environmental sustainability disclosure? UK evidence. *Business Strategy and the Environment, 26*(8), 1061–1077.

Kreander, N., & McPhail, K. (2019). State investments and human rights? The case of the Norwegian government pension fund global. *Accounting, Auditing & Accountability Journal, 32*(6), 1742–1770.

Krippendorff, K. (2018). *Content analysis*. Sage Publication.

Kun, A. (2018). How to operationalize open norms in hard and soft laws: Reflections based on two distinct regulatory examples. *International Journal of Comparative Labour Law and Industrial Relations, 34*(1), 23–51.

Lauwo, S., & Otusanya, O. J. (2014). Corporate accountability and human rights disclosures: A case study of Barrick Gold Mine in Tanzania. *Accounting Forum, 38*(2), 91–108.

Le Luo, L., & Tang, Q. (2016). Does national culture influence corporate carbon disclosure propensity? *Journal of International Accounting Research, 15*(1), 17–47.

Leopizzi, R., Iazzi, A., Venturelli, A., & Principale, S. (2020). Nonfinancial risk disclosure: The "state of the art" of Italian companies. *Corporate Social Responsibility and Environmental Management, 27*(1), 358–368.

Liu, Y. S., & Yang, J. H. (2018). A longitudinal analysis of corporate greenhouse gas disclosure strategy. *Corporate Governance (Bingley), 18*(2), 317–330.

Mahoney, L. S., Thorne, L., Cecil, L., & LaGore, W. (2013). A research note on standalone corporate social responsibility reports: Signaling or greenwashing? *Critical Perspectives on Accounting, 24*(4–5), 350–359.

Mallin, C. A., & Michelon, G. (2011). Board reputation attributes and corporate social performance: An empirical investigation of the US best corporate citizens. *Accounting and Business Research, 41*(2), 119–144.

Matuszak, Ł., & Różańska, E. (2021). Towards 2014/95/EU directive compliance: The case of Poland. *Sustainability Accounting, Management and Policy Journal, 12*(5), 1052–1076.

McPhail, K., & Ferguson, J. (2016). The past, the present and the future of accounting for human rights. *Accounting, Auditing and Accountability Journal, 29*(4), 526–541.

McPhail, K., Macdonald, K., & Ferguson, J. (2016). Should the international accounting standards board have responsibility for human rights? *Accounting, Auditing & Accountability Journal, 29*(4), 594–616.

Muchlinski, P. (2012). Implementing the new UN corporate human rights framework: Implications for corporate law, governance, and regulation. *Business Ethics Quarterly, 22*(1), 145–177.

Munasinghe, A., Cuckston, T., & Rowbottom, N. (2021). Sustainability certification as marketisation: Rainforest alliance in the Sri Lankan tea production industry. *Accounting Forum, 45*(3), 247–272.

Muttakin, M. B., Khan, A., & Mihret, D. G. (2018). The effect of board capital and CEO power on corporate social responsibility disclosures. *Journal of Business Ethics, 150*(1), 41–56.

Onida, P. (1971). *Economia d'azienda*. UTET.

Panfilo, S., & Krasodomska, J. (2022). Climate change risk disclosure in Europe: The role of cultural-cognitive, regulative, and normative factors. *Accounting in Europe*, 1–28.

Paoloni, P., Lombardi, R., & Principale, S. (2023). The impact of gender diversity on corporate social responsibility knowledge: Empirical analysis in European context. *Journal of Knowledge Management.*

Parsa, S., Roper, I., Muller-Camen, M., & Szigetvari, E. (2018). Have labour practices and human rights disclosures enhanced corporate accountability? The case of the GRI framework. *Accounting Forum, 42*(1), 47–64.

Pianezzi, D., Cinquini, L., Grossi, G., & Sargiacomo, M. (2022, April). Migration and the neoliberal state: Accounting ethics in the Italian response to the refugee crisis. *Accounting Forum, 46*(2), 134–159). Routledge.

Pizzi, S., Del Baldo, M., Caputo, F., & Venturelli, A. (2022a). Voluntary disclosure of sustainable development goals in mandatory non-financial reports: The moderating role of cultural dimension. *Journal of International Financial Management and Accounting, 33*(1), 83–106.

Pizzi, S., Principale, S., & de Nuccio, E. (2022b). Material sustainability information and reporting standards. Exploring the differences between GRI and SASB. *Meditari Accountancy Research.*

Sannino, G., Lucchese, M., Zampone, G., & Lombardi, R. (2020). Cultural dimensions, global reporting initiatives commitment, and corporate social responsibility issues: New evidence from organisation for economic co-operation and development banks. *Corporate Social Responsibility and Environmental Management, 27*(4), 1653–1663.

Sherman, J., & Lehr, A. (2010). *Human rights due diligence: Is it too risky*. Corporate social responsibility initiative working paper, 55.

Spedding, L. S. (2005). *Due diligence and corporate governance*. Elsevier Science.

Ullah, S., Adams, K., Adams, D., & Attah-Boakye, R. (2021). Multinational corporations and human right violations in emerging economies: Do commitment to social and environmental responsibility matter? *Journal of Environmental Management, 280.*

UN. (2018). UN guiding principles on business and human rights: Implementing the United Nations "protect, respect and remedy" framework, 2011. In *International human rights law documents* (pp. 348–354).

van der Ploeg, L., & Vanclay, F. (2017). A tool for improving the management of social and human rights risks at project sites: The Human Rights Sphere. *Journal of Cleaner Production, 142*, 4072–4084.

Veprauskaite, E., & Adams, M. (2013). Do powerful chief executives influence the financial performance of UK firms? *The British Accounting Review, 45*(3), 229–241.

Vigneau, L., Humphreys, M., & Moon, J. (2015). How do firms comply with international sustainability standards? Processes and consequences of adopting the global reporting initiative. *Journal of Business Ethics, 131*(2), 469–486.

Wang, Z., & Sarkis, J. (2017). Corporate social responsibility governance, outcomes, and financial performance. *Journal of Cleaner Production, 162*, 1607–1616.

Zeng, X., Momin, M., & Nurunnabi, M. (2022). Photo disclosure in human rights issues by fortune companies: An impression management perspective. *Sustainability Accounting, Management and Policy Journal, 13*(3), 568–599.

Chapter 5
Conclusion Remark

Keywords Due diligence · Corporate sustainability due diligence · Corporate governance · Human rights

5.1 First Results on Sustainable Corporate Governance and Due Diligence

The last decade has been characterized by the awareness of the importance of sustainability. Global warming, the increase in extreme weather events, the pandemic and wars have exponentially highlighted the importance of sustainability and the relevance for communities to take organized actions aimed at achieving the objectives of the 2030 Agenda. Therefore, sustainability from a topic debated only among scholars it has now become relevant also for organizations and companies.

This book investigates the close relationship between corporate governance and sustainability by analyzing the proposed Due Diligence Directive, the first European regulatory intervention towards sustainable corporate governance. Before going into the details of the legislative proposal, it was deemed necessary to start from the analysis of the scientific studies on the topic and investigate the frontier thematic strands. Academics have emphasized the relevance of governance for improving sustainability performance and achieving the Sustainable Development Goals. The analysis of the literature in recent years has shown three main trends: (a) composition of corporate governance; (b) governance and accountability; (c) corporate governance and sustainability reporting. Governance responsibility must be a lever to improve performance and sustainability disclosure.

In this regard, the choices of the European Commission are aimed at increasing the accountability and transparency of information (as for the NFRD). The proposed Directive on Due Diligence aims to stimulate the action of companies in favor of an increase in information credibility and commitment by governance. The proposal was welcomed by various categories of stakeholders and organizations who believe that a more stringent regulation of human rights Due Diligence would bring benefits both in practices and in sustainable communication. This first proposal envisages greater obligations and responsibilities for directors and identifies the procedures

S. Principale, *Fostering Sustainability in Corporate Governance*, SIDREA Series in Accounting and Business Administration,
https://doi.org/10.1007/978-3-031-30354-8_5

that companies should adopt so that human rights are respected in the value chain, including the supply chain.

Finally, it has been shown how little widespread human rights due diligence procedures are among European public interest entities. The results presented in the fourth chapter show that only 14% of the large companies analyzed have implemented due diligence procedures. These data are in support of those who have welcomed the proposal of the European Commission. The quantitative analysis was aimed at identifying the drivers on which companies can leverage to absorb good practices in the field of human rights more quickly. Among the various characteristics, the presence of the CSR committee and the separation of roles between CEO and chairman are the characteristics that have had the greatest impact on corporate good practices.

5.2 Corporate Governance Challenges and Future Perspectives

Academics, international organizations, regulators, and practitioners all agree that governance is central to the integration of sustainability in the company and for the ecological transition of the economy. Corporate social responsibility, therefore, requires a change from the traditional models of maximizing profits for shareholders. Over the years, these models have led companies to continuously ignore social and environmental issues as they are concentrated on achieving profit in the short term. Currently it is no longer conceivable that such models can be valid even with the current conditions of the economy and the competitive environment.

It is believed that, in addition to changes in business models in favor of models that take strong account of sustainability paradigms, governance mechanisms also need to be reformed. The company whose board of directors deals with environmental, social, and governance issues or a governance that gives more space to the will of the stakeholders should no longer be an isolated case. Governance must be ready for the challenges that sustainability imposes to face and must be ready for the continuous changes of the external environment, which is increasingly changeable and discontinuous.

Therefore, increasingly specific skills are required within the various levels of governance. The due diligence covered in this book or even non-financial reporting are some examples of how much governance needs to be updated and have the requisites to understand the new matter. For the best strategic decisions to be taken, governance must have the skills to interpret ESG information and implement effective and consistent responses to related issues. To date, governance must be able to combine adequate levels of profitability with activities that guarantee sustainable development. It should be considered that the financial markets, especially the EU ones, tend more and more towards more stringent regulation in the ESG area and increasingly require more information and fulfilments. Listed companies will be called increasingly overexposed to ESG regulation.

Governance must respond to the challenge relating to the speed of changes in the external environment. The proposed legislation on Sustainable Corporate Governance is just one of the future legislation that will be introduced and to which companies will be called to respond.

Finally, it should be noted that the greater structuring of governance models is not a univocal answer. The presence of greater or lesser levels of the governance structure is not always a successful and necessary element for optimal strategic management. Each company has its own peculiarities that differentiate it from the others. Therefore, a uniformity of governance systems may not be an optimal solution, considering the uniqueness of companies for internal characteristics and contextual factors. Good governance must be able to find the optimal answers by identifying the governance model that is closest to its nature. This would make it possible to clarify good strategic governance aimed at harmonizing the relationship between the company and the stakeholders in order to stimulate a virtuous circle aimed at increasing corporate value.

Printed by Printforce, the Netherlands